"Robert Sharpe, Sr.'s book stands out because of its exceptional simplicity. It provides essential information which givers, as well as volunteer and professional fund raisers, must have in order to choose the most appropriate and efficient method of giving. It explains gift planning opportunities in simple terms, while advising when the complexities require the help of a qualified gift planner."

—David R. Dunlop
Former Senior Development Officer
Cornell University

"This is the only source I am aware of that addresses the *who* and *why* as well as the *what*, *when*, and *how* of gift giving. Mr. Sharpe articulates so well the roles that *emotion* and *intellect* play in the gift-giving process. This book is relevant to all of us who are part of the exciting drama of giving—givers, volunteers, gift planners, advisors, and institutional leaders."

—Laird Yock
Rochester, MN

"Many will benefit from this comprehensive planned giving primer . . . a fine piece of work by possibly the most qualified professional in the industry."

—Bob Shelby
Manager of Field Services
Billy Graham Evangelistic Association

"In his new book Bob Sharpe, Sr. advises us to put the needs of givers to give before those of gift planners and the institutions for which they work. His advice to put the needs of those who give first is made more valuable knowing it comes from someone who has trained thousands of nonprofit institution gift planners."

—Gid Smith
President
Community Foundation of Greater Memphis

"Reading Robert F. Sharpe, Sr.'s book *Planned Giving Simplified: The Gift, the Giver, and the Gift Planner* is like watching a magician reveal the long-held mysteries of his profession. As the CEO of a growing not-for-profit organization which must raise $3 million a year, there are days I can hardly face asking anyone else for money. Sharpe's book, however, has invigorated me to spend more concerted effort on cultivating planned gifts. He's made the whole process seem more manageable."

—G. Scott Morris, MD, Executive Director
The Church Health Center
Memphis, TN

# PLANNED GIVING SIMPLIFIED

## The Gift, the Giver, and the Gift Planner

**Robert F. Sharpe, Sr.**

**John Wiley & Sons, Inc.**
New York • Chichester • Weinheim • Brisbane • Singapore • Toronto

In appreciation for what the 18 members of my family mean to me, I dedicate this book to them: My wife, Jane Allen Sharpe; Susan Sharpe Hedge; Dwight Lamar Hedge; Laura Jane Hedge; Paul Dwight Hedge; Robert F. Sharpe, Jr.; Donna Ernstine Sharpe; Emily Houston Sharpe; Elizabeth Noble Sharpe; Paul Allen Sharpe; Beverly Massey Sharpe; Justin Massey Sharpe; Hunter Hillman Sharpe; Grayson Gates Sharpe; Timothy David Sharpe; Alison Quin; Rosemary Jane Sharpe; and Colin Quin Sharpe.

This book is printed on acid-free paper. ∞

Copyright © 1999 by Robert F. Sharpe, Sr. All rights reserved.

Published by John Wiley & Sons, Inc.
Published simultaneously in Canada.

This publication is designed to provide accurate and authoritative information in regard to the subject matter covered. It is sold with the understanding that the publisher is not engaged in rendering professional services. If professional advice or other expert assistance is required, the services of a competent professional person should be sought.

*Library of Congress Cataloging-in-Publication Data:*

Sharpe, Robert.
    Planned giving simplified : the gift, the giver, and the gift planner / Robert F. Sharpe, Sr.
        p.   cm.—(The NSFRE/Wiley fund development series)
    Includes bibliographical references and index.
    ISBN 0-471-16674-X (cloth : alk. paper)
    1. Deferred giving—United States.   I. Title.   II. Series.
HV41.9.U5S523   1998
355.15'224—dc21                                                    98-24360

Printed in the United States of America.

10 9 8 7 6 5 4 3 2

There is dignity in simplicity.
                    —Margaret, the Lady Thatcher,
                    Former Prime Minister of
                    Great Britain and the 21st
                    Chancellor of the College of
                    William and Mary

*The NSFRE/Wiley Fund Development Series*

The NSFRE/Wiley Fund Development Series is intended to provide fund development professionals, volunteers including board members (and others interested in the not-for-profit sector) with top-quality publications that help advance philanthropy as voluntary action for the public good. Our goal is to provide practical, timely guidance and information on fund raising, charitable giving, and related subjects. NSFRE and Wiley each bring to this innovative collaboration unique and important resources that result in a whole greater than the sum of its parts.

## The National Society of Fund Raising Executives

The NSFRE is a professional association of fund-raising executives that advances philanthropy through its more than 18,000 members in 145 chapters throughout the United States, Canada, and Mexico. Through its advocacy, research, education, and certification programs, the Society fosters development and growth of fund-raising professionals, works to advance philanthropy and volunteerism, and promotes high ethical standards in the fund-raising profession.

## 1997–1998 NSFRE Publishing Advisory Council

Nina P. Berkheiser, CFRE
Society for the Prevention of Cruelty to Animals of Pinellas County
St. Petersburg, Florida

Linda L. Chew, CFRE
Director, Major Gifts, Alta Bates Foundation

Samuel N. Gough, CFRE
Washington, DC

Suzanne Hittman, CFRE
Chair, Fund Raising Counsel

Ann R. Hyatt, ACFRE
Director of Development/Alumni Relations, Pace University School of
    Law

Marie A. Reed, Ed.D., CNAA
Vice President, Professional Advancement, National Society of Fund
    Raising Executives

James A. Reid, Ph.D., CFRE
Principal Consultant, Philanthropic Resource Associates

G. Patrick Williams, M.S., ACFRE
President/CEO, Lourdes College Foundation

# About the Author

Robert F. Sharpe, Sr. is the founder of Robert F. Sharpe and Company, Inc., a firm based in Memphis, Tennessee, that provides instruction and support services to the leadership of nonprofit organizations as they plan, market, manage, and evaluate their planned giving programs. He founded the consulting business in 1963, after working for ten years in the life insurance business, followed by positions as the Secretary of Stewardship at the Good News Broadcasting Association, and executive director of the Evangelical Presbyterian Foundation.

In 1967, Robert F. Sharpe, Sr. founded the National Planned Giving Institute—now the National Planned Giving Institute at the College of William and Mary—which was transferred as a planned gift in 1993 to the college by Robert F. Sharpe and Company, Inc. During its 32-year history the Institute has received more than 28,000 individual seminar registrations. Mr. Sharpe continues to serve as the executive director and as a trustee of the Endowment Association of the College of William and Mary.

In addition to speaking and training, Mr. Sharpe has written hundreds of booklets, brochures, newsletters, articles, and ads on charitable gift planning which have been used by thousands of nonprofit institutions on subjects designed to inform, motivate, and educate prospective planned givers. He authored the books *27 Plus Ways to Increase Giving to Your Church*, *The Planned Giving Idea Book*, and *Everything You Need to Know Before You Give Another Dime*. His articles have appeared in such national publications as *Fund Raising Management*, *CASE Currents*, *Advancing Philanthropy*, *Planned Giving Today*, and others.

Mr. Sharpe has been married to his wife, Jane, for 50 years, and they have four children and nine grandchildren.

# Contents

# Foreword

In 1959 when my father began his career in what was then known as *deferred giving*, this method of providing resources to fund philanthropic endeavors was little understood. The use of charitable bequests, gift annuities, and charitable trusts had a rich history in Europe and America (the American Council on Gift Annuities was, for example, founded in 1927), but in the boom years of postwar America these plans had become a relatively unimportant part of fund raising in this country, and few people had taken the time and effort to truly understand their proper use.

Only a small number of charitable organizations and institutions employed persons who specialized in working with donors to complete what are today known as *planned gifts*. Few resources were available to my father and others who were left largely to their own devices as they worked to build planned gift development programs aimed at helping donors make their gifts in the most effective ways for them, their loved ones, and the charities they wished to benefit.

During the 1950s and 1960s, charitable trusts and other gift vehicles were, however, being utilized by some advisors outside the charitable community as tax-avoidance techniques, with apparently little thought given to the philanthropic element of the process. This activity was widespread enough to draw the attention of Congressional tax-writing committees, and culminated in the landmark legislation known as the Tax Reform Act of 1969. This legislation placed significant restrictions on the use of charitable remainder trusts, pooled income funds, and other *split interest* gifts in the planning of charitable gifts.

While intended to curb abuses in the area of charitable gift planning, an unfortunate myth developed over time that the 1969 tax legislation actually invented planned giving. While this was not true (my father labored in this field for a decade prior to the 1969 act), nevertheless there began a long period of confusion about the origin and nature of charitable gift planning that still continues to this day.

Because of mind numbing complexities the 1969 Act brought to the charitable tax planning process, during the 1970s a cottage industry sprang up based around the explanation of this act. Many of the early service providers had their roots in tax planning and trust marketing. Not surprisingly, therefore, what might be considered an inordinate emphasis was placed by many on the tax aspects of charitable giving, even to the point of belief that tax motivations were the primary cause for larger charitable gifts!

In the wake of the new complexities ushered in by the 1969 Tax Act, many organizations began adding specialists to their staff who were at the time known as directors of deferred giving. In some cases these persons, while they were quite knowledgeable and eager to practice their craft, were isolated from the mainstream of fund development. In many organizations, it was perceived that they were involved in an alien activity that was not really a part of fund raising.

From the earliest stages of his career, my father labored to maintain the balance between the tax and financial motivations inherent in charitable gift planning vehicles and the deeper, more complex motivators at the very root of this behavior. Our company continues that emphasis today.

Because he began his career in the financial services industry, he was keenly aware of the multitude of motivations underlying the financial and estate planning process and how they could sometimes seem at odds with and frustrate the desire of even the most highly motivated persons to make meaningful charitable gifts. As he made the transition to working to assist nonprofit organizations and institutions build long-term economic security through encouraging larger gifts, he was quickly convinced that for most persons the only way to complete gifts of a magnitude that could effect the financial security of the donor was to structure them in such a way as to assure that very economic freedom and security.

In the early 1970s it was difficult, if not impossible, for a donor or a charity to find an advisor who was competent to assist in the completion of a planned gift, regardless of how much the donor might wish to give. The passage of the 1969 Tax Reform Act had killed the interest of many for-profit advisors in charitable giving as a tax planning technique as most decided it was not worth the investment of time and energy to master the complexities of the 1969 Act. It was, therefore, left to the charities themselves to master these techniques and provide assistance to those who wished to make gifts in this manner.

The period from 1970 to 1986 was a time of great expansion of charitable gift planning efforts that were rooted in specialized programs that were part of the fund development efforts of many American charities, especially among the ranks of higher education, healthcare, and larger religious organizations. The growth in planned gifts during this period was primarily in the area of charitable bequests. An economic environment characterized by high interest rates, inflation, and long-term negative returns in investment markets was not conducive to the effective use of gift annuities, charitable remainder trusts, and most other gift planning tools that were based on irrevocable transfers of assets with various financial benefits reserved for the donors.

Today, we are over a decade into a revolution in charitable gift planning that began with the landmark tax legislation enacted in 1986. This legislation dramatically increased capital gains taxes and, in so doing, increased the attractiveness of charitable remainder trusts and other planning tools that could be used to help avoid, minimize, or delay the imposition of this tax. The aging of the American donor population and unprecedented increases in asset values in an environment of low interest rates and inflation has also greatly increased the attractiveness of various gift planning techniques.

As a result, many of the leading financial services providers today are approaching their clients and initiating the planning of charitable remainder trusts and other gifts with or without the knowledge or participation of the ultimate charitable beneficiary. While recent legislation has reduced the tax benefits of charitable remainder trusts by building upon the restrictions of the 1969 Act and subsequent legislation, charitable gift planning still offers significant tax and financial benefits to many wealthy Americans who have charitable interests that they would like to combine with wise tax and investment planning. This activity is creating an unprecedented number of charitable remainder trusts and other vehicles that help donors effectively meld together their charitable and personal financial planning interests.

Ironically, however, the vastly increased knowledge of and interest in planned giving techniques among financial advisors in recent years has brought us full circle. As the capability to complete planned gifts is more widespread, and any number of organizations in both the nonprofit and for-profit world can offer individuals the benefits of these plans, the difference between whether or not plans are actually implemented increasingly lies within the understanding of the gift that must precede the plan.

There is no shortage of information on the technical aspects of planned giving. That, however, is not the purpose of this book. The real challenge in planned giving is in knowing what to do after you understand how the plans work—that is the price of entry into the world of charitable gift planning today. Vastly more challenging is understanding the nature of the persons who make planned gifts, and the motivations that lead them to choose to complete essentially the same gift from a technical standpoint for the benefit of one organization rather than another.

Planners who understand the who and why of the planning process will be the ones who make it to the point of discussing the what, when, and how of the gift. Those who think they can still romance the what, when, and how to the point that it becomes the why and uncovers the who may well find this approach less effective in an era of more widespread knowledge.

Likewise, those who believe they can simply pay lip service to charitable motivations before getting to the "real benefits" for the donor will find that donors and clients will see through this approach and choose instead to turn to those who truly understand their philanthropic impulses.

This book will be of value to the for-profit and nonprofit planner alike. For the reader from the nonprofit world, it represents a comprehensive overview of the body of knowledge and skills that must be brought to bear to succeed in helping donors plan gifts more effectively. For the reader from the for-profit sector, this book will be an excellent insight into the world of planned giving from the perspective of the nonprofits that must increasingly depend on this source of gift support in future years.

The title of this book, *Planned Giving Simplified*, should be understood in the context in which it is intended. Charitable gift planning is, in fact, an enormously complex enterprise when taken in its entirety. The process requires knowledge of every conceivable type of property a donor may own, the numerous forms in which it may be held, the myriad possibilities for transferring it to both charitable and noncharitable beneficiaries, the estate settlement process, federal and state tax and securities laws, state insurance regulation, state laws regulating fund raising, and any number of other bodies of knowledge.

In addition, the successful gift planner must understand all of the various motivations underlying the desire to make charitable gifts. These can involve emotional considerations, political and economic theory, social theory, and an understanding of the full range of religious beliefs that are the foundation of many persons' desire to give.

It is obvious that few persons have ever, or will ever, master all aspects of the gift planning process. This book recognizes that fact and proceeds from that premise and concludes that only a team effort comprised of many persons who understand their role and that of others involved will be successful.

In *Planned Giving Simplified*, the reader will find a comprehensive approach based on a lifetime of experience to help guide them in further exploration of the subject, and one that should be extremely helpful to those who would like to understand the character and dimension of the forest before they embark on a study of the many types of trees that comprise it.

Robert F. Sharpe, Jr.
Memphis, TN

# Preface

The concept behind this book is simple. Planned giving is people (givers) doing what they want to do with their assets and gift planners helping them do it.

Some complex ideas, techniques, and personalities are behind this simple statement. We will look at the gift, which may be made in many ways, from simple to complicated. Then we'll consider the people who give, why they give, what they give to fund their gifts, the timing of the gifts, and how gifts are completed. Finally we'll focus on the gift planners and their role in the charitable gift-planning process. I hope this book will help take some of the mystery out of planned giving. Too often people think planned giving is a highly technical subject that only a few people can fathom. I also hope to convince trustees, senior management, and those responsible for establishing planned giving programs that their charitable gift planner doesn't have to become a specialist in tax law. To be effective, charitable gift planners have to become specialists in human relations. I once heard someone say, "It is usually cheaper to buy a service, than learn it and keep abreast of it every day. Regardless of the cost, you will probably be better served if you buy the information from experts on an as-needed basis." Thus, rather than gift planners trying to learn enough about tax law to give opinions, it is probably less costly for them to learn enough to talk about taxes and then buy the tax services needed from those who specialize in tax law.

As these subjects are discussed, keep in mind that I am writing from the perspective that people have a built-in need to give. Givers want to help other people; they believe that when they give to charities, they are indirectly helping committed people carry out the stated mission of the institution.

By built-in need to give, I mean that giving is the outward response to an inward need people have to express appreciation, gratefulness, satisfaction, and joy through giving. Careful giving expresses who we are and why we are what we are as individuals; it helps us to perpetuate our values. The idea of making major current and/or deferred planned gifts, I believe, almost always begins in the seat of our emotions. The *who* and *why* parts of the gift process deal with the emotions. Yet even though major current and deferred planned gifts are emotional experiences, rarely are they made without the approval of the intellect, which deals with the *what, when*, and *how* parts of the gift process.

People give because they want to give. As people grow older, they are more interested in receiving help to plan their giving carefully. Through careful planning, their gifts can be more productive, and the people can keep their financial security and maintain their economic freedom. Charitable gift planners can help prospective planned givers by offering to coordinate the gift-planning process and by working with them and those of their advisors who need to become involved in the charitable estate gift-planning process. Charitable gift-planning executives sometimes act as coordinators of the charitable estate- and gift-planning process for key donors.

In order to serve their donors, charitable institutions must develop carefully planned giving programs. To be successful, such programs must be planned carefully and committed to by the institutional leadership. The board of trustees and chief executive officer (CEO) of the institution are key ingredients in any successful planned giving program. The leadership of every institution needs to ask and answer the following questions before launching a planned giving program. Coincidentally, these are the very questions I hope this book answers.

- What is a planned gift?
- Why is a planned giving program necessary?
- How will it benefit the institution?
- What will it cost and when will it "pay off"?
- How does it fit into the overall mission of the institution?
- Where will prospective planned givers be found and how much time will be required of the board of trustees, the CEO, and other management people for the program to succeed?
- What can be expected in deferred gifts if an institution does not have a planned giving program?
- How much annual budget will be needed to secure planned gifts? . . . and for how long?

Through charitable gift planning, gift planners can help people become good stewards by showing them ways to give the same amount at less cost or give more without increasing their cost of giving. For example, when prospective planned givers own appreciated securities and want to make a gift, giving securities rather than cash will almost always save them money in taxes. In addition, because a planned giving program is an organized plan that encourages people to include the institution in their wills or other estate-planning documents, income to the organization eventually increases.

Planned giving benefits the institution because new gifts will be discovered, and those people who are giving now will be shown how to give more effectively, which is likely to result in larger gifts.

The cost of planned giving efforts will vary by the kind of program adopted and by the age and type of institution. Generally speaking, institutions just initiating planned giving programs can expect the budget for the first year to be at least twice the salary of the planned giving officer, give or take 10 percent, plus the cost of employing secretarial staff and paying the office overhead. In future years the increased budget should be covered by increased income. When planned giving is defined to include both current and deferred gifts, the program should begin to produce results in a few months. Deferred planned gifts usually will commence maturing, as the direct result and effort of the planned giving executive, within three to seven years, depending on the type of institution and the average age of the constituents. Sometimes it is difficult to trace matured planned gifts to the efforts expended by recently employed planned giving staff members during the early years of the program's existence. In most well-established institutions, there will be earlier maturities, but a careful investigation usually reveals that those managing the new planned giving program rarely had any contact with early deferred gift maturities. These maturities very likely resulted because those in charge of the institution did something right before the planned giving program was established.

Planned giving programs must fit into the overall mission of the institution. Those in charge of the program render a needed service to present and future givers who want to make major current and/or deferred planned gifts to this and other institutions. I mention other institutions deliberately because generally people also desire to give to other institutions. Givers almost always give more to the institution whose charitable gift planner is assisting them in the planned giving process. My experience has been that planned giving programs ought not to be designed to "get people's money" to fund the mission of their institution but rather to "help people give" to fund the mission of the institution(s) of their choice. Most prospective planned givers are already in the files of the charitable institutions and are likely long-term or former givers. Many are small regular givers whose current assets will be well under the amount required for filing federal estate and gift tax returns. In fact, most bequests I have worked with have been made by people whose total estates were valued at less than $500,000.

The question of how much management time will be required if the program is to be successful will depend on who does what. Apart from several things that the executive director, board members, business office staff, and others must do, duties can be handled in various ways. One of the first questions to be answered is whether the institution can legally act as trustee of trusts created by their donors.

Sometimes institutions without planned giving programs receive a few bequests from wills and an occasional maturity of a trust the institutions didn't know about. While the regular flow of deferred gifts will come primarily from wills, some gifts will be received through other estate-planning vehicles.

The planned giving program needs to be executed by a charitable gift planner on staff who accepts the position on the basis that he or she will remain in the position for at least five years. It takes that long for most planned giving executives to see very many deferred gifts mature because of the death of individuals with whom they had worked directly.

I don't like to use the term "fund raisers" when referring to those who work in planned giving because securing major planned gifts is not the usual fund-raising activity. After working for nearly four decades as an employee of nonprofit organizations and as a consultant, writer, and teacher in the world of planned giving, I have concluded that some people who refer to themselves as fund raisers are not really the fund raisers at all. They are fund *gatherers*, or those who harvest. They reap where others have sown. Without the program people, planned giving executives do not have a case to present to prospective planned givers. It seems to me that the real fund raisers are the program people who carry out the mission of the institution.

This is not a how-to book, taking the reader step-by-step through the mechanics of starting and building planned giving programs. Rather it represents my attempt at applying some 40 years of experience in this arena to all players in the gift-planning drama. After reading it, everyone—givers, gift planners, financial advisors, leaders of institutions—should have an idea of what can be done to execute more effective planned giving programs in charitable institutions.

Robert F. Sharpe, Sr.
Memphis, TN

# Acknowledgments

Margaret, the Lady Thatcher, former Prime Minister of Great Britain and the twenty-first chancellor of the College of William and Mary, speaking recently in Williamsburg, Virginia, stated: "There is dignity in simplicity." This statement was the seed implanted in my mind that led me to select the title for this book, *Planned Giving Simplified: The Gift, the Giver, and the Gift Planner.*

This book started with a telephone call from Marla Bobowick, who was then an editor at John Wiley & Sons, Inc. She gave me guidance and helped me get started before leaving for further study.

Martha Cooley became my able editor, and I do mean able. She gave me invaluable help, put up with my jump starts on a subject, and continued to help and smile when I made a sudden 180-degree turn in thought. She was patient. Thanks, Martha.

Jane Allen Sharpe, my wife, editor, and mentor, has been vital to me as we have worked together for 50 years. She has listened and has been my critic for decades. Without her, this book would not have been possible.

Ruth Hones, one of my favorite people of all time and former vice president and editor at Robert F. Sharpe and Co., Inc., was a godsend. She has edited most of my writings for

ACKNOWLEDGMENTS

15 years. She has a great understanding of planned giving and has been helpful in writing this book. Ruth played a vital role and made it possible for me to submit the finished manuscript.

Many others have had a part in the completion of this book. Lonnie Faulkner helped me keep moving ahead many times. Her presence, her countenance, and her quiet encouragement kept me on course.

The thousands of people who have attended the National Planned Giving Institute at the College of William and Mary since 1967 have taught me much of what I have written.

Institute faculty members—John Watts for 26 years, Alan Cates for 20 years, Jonathon Tidd for 17 years, and Donna Palmer for 20 years—have been teaching me all these years. Probably more than any others, they have helped me prepare for writing this book. John Watts, has advised me and been my friend for nearly 40 years, read this manuscript in the early stages and made an important contribution. Donna Palmer, who has been a severe but important critic, challenged me concerning content and insisted on clarity. She carefully reviewed all of the trial manuscripts of this book and finally okayed it.

Tom Cullinan and Tom Dyer, both lawyers, read the manuscript in the early stages and were helpful with financial and legal content.

Stewart Gamage, Barbara Greinke, Samuel Jones, Charles Mamonies, Nancy Nash, Dean Olson, Lois Parker, Dennis Slon, Debra Vick, William Walker, and Mary Ann Williamson from the College of William and Mary have directly and indirectly contributed to the preparation of this book.

So many people at Robert F. Sharpe and Company assisted me in the preparation of this book. Thanks to Phillip Adcock, Darlene Grissom, Vickie Hargett, Nancy Jeffers, Barlow Mann, Bo McElroy, Cindy Parrish, Kathy Robbins, Mark Romer, Stephanie Rossi, Timothy Sharpe, Robert

**xxviii**

Sharpe, Jr., Caleen Williams, and others whose help has been invaluable.

I am in debt to the management and trustees of hundreds of charitable institutions and organizations with whom I have consulted throughout my career. Writing this book would have been impossible had I not had the opportunity to work with and learn from you.

I asked friends in the legal, banking and trusts, financial planning, accounting, community foundation, and charitable institutions of all kinds for help and advice.

My thanks to my friend Thomas Dyer, Esquire, for writing a section of the book about the role of lawyers in the charitable estate- and gift-planning process.

I appreciate many others who helped me stay on track. Burns Landis, CFP, reviewed the text concerning financial planning. Gid Smith helped with what I wrote about community foundations. Robert Booth made helpful suggestions about financial service companies. Kirk Bailey and John Temple reviewed what I wrote about the role of trust companies in the charitable estate- and gift-planning process. Kenneth Plunk and Douglas Noble helped me clarify what I wrote about a corporate planned gift. Timothy Wheat, CPA, helped me as I wrote about what certified public accountants can do to help people complete major current and/or deferred planned gifts and to Dee Dyer for help in research.

As I thought about writing this book, I felt there was a need to reach out beyond planned giving. As a result, I asked: William T. Wolf to relate his views on philanthropy, Dr. Timothy J. Sullivan to discuss public service, Rabbi Marc Lee Raphael to write about *Tsedakah*, Dr. Robert G. den Dulk to discuss giving from the Christian perspective, Dr. Tullia Brown Hamilton to discuss philanthropy and voluntarism in the Black community, and Dr. Robert Gross to bring the history of giving in early America to the book.

ACKNOWLEDGMENTS

Their essays help to complete this book and makes it more valuable to those interested in volunteerism. I am grateful to each of them for their contribution.

I believe that Stewardship + *Tsedakah* + Philanthropy + Public Service = Volunteerism. This, to me, is true because all of us are involved in any part of volunteerism have been influenced to give time, knowledge, and money because of what we learned in our homes and in institutions that have been funded by voluntary givers.

It is impossible for me to bring to my remembrance all the people I am indebted to for making this book a reality. I regret it if I have failed to show appreciation to anyone.

# **I** THE PLANNED GIFT

A planned gift can be defined as "a voluntary gift of any kind, in any amount, given for any purpose—operations, capital expansion, or endowment—either current or deferred, when the assistance of a qualified volunteer, professional staff person, or the giver's own advisor(s) is needed to help complete the gift. This section of the book deals with the planned gift itself.

A gift is an outward expression of appreciation, gratitude, satisfaction, and joy. Giving expresses who we are and why we give. Giving is an emotional response.

Planned giving includes the who, why, what, when, and how of giving. What we give, when we give, and how we make major current and deferred planned gifts is the work of the intellect.

Both the emotions and the intellect are involved in all planned gift decisions. The idea of giving originates in the emotions, the who and why. The intellect decides what, when, and how the gift is to be made.

# 1  An Introduction to Planned Gifts

Making a gift is an act of voluntarily transferring something one possesses to another without expecting anything in return. The gift becomes a tax-deductible charitable gift when it is delivered to a qualified tax-exempt institution. People make either planned or unplanned charitable gifts. Unplanned gifts are made without much thought and are often small. Examples of this can be anything from tossing a dollar in the collection bucket of a street Santa to writing a $100 check after being touched emotionally by a charity's mailing. Planned gifts usually are completed after considerable thought on the part of the donor and are given for any purpose that serves the mission of the organization—operations, capital expansion, or endowment. While these gifts can be of any amount, they are often large. A large gift is whatever the giver considers larger than what they normally give. Each institution will determine what it considers a large gift. Many charitable institutions receive up to one-third of their total gift income from 10 or fewer sources. A source can be defined as any individual current gift, including deferred gifts maturing in that year, grants made by foundations, sponsorships, corporations, and/or support from other entities.

Givers often work through the gift-planning process with someone they trust—often a financial or legal professional—who helps them determine the size of the gift, whether the gift is to be made currently or to be deferred, how it is funded (with cash or other assets), any restrictions as to use, and finally, the tax implications of the gift. An important point to keep in mind is that planned gifts can be for current or deferred use. Current gifts are given outright and usually consist of cash, securities, or other gifts or assets. The charitable institution will receive deferred gifts at some future date during life or after the death of the giver. Deferred gifts can be made to charitable institutions in wills, trusts, and other estate-planning documents and in most cases will be revocable, meaning that the giver can take back all or part of the gift upon revocation of the gift arrangement. As a rule people do not make wills or estate plans just to make a deferred gift; rather, the gift is made in conjunction with other estate planning.

Deferred gifts are not included in the top-10 or fewer gift category until the year they mature. However, it is important to some executives to have an idea of the real value of deferred gifts completed during the year. While the Financial Accounting Standards Board (FASB) rules may be good for accounting purposes, I lean toward the idea of not counting revocable gift arrangements until they mature but carefully acknowledging and recognizing anyone who states that your institution is a beneficiary through any revocable arrangement.

A special point to note as you read this book: Current tax advice is available from many legal and financial sources. Therefore the planned gift arrangements discussed in this book are general in nature, and specific tax information is not included. Readers should contact tax counsel for specific information concerning the tax implications of any plan of giving.

## WHAT PEOPLE GIVE TO FUND PLANNED GIFTS

People spend the greater part of their lives working and learning how to earn, save, conserve, accumulate, preserve, and distribute property. Property is a most important and interesting subject to all who give.

It is vital for charitable gift planners to understand financial security, economic freedom, and the "time value" of money. What older people think about these issues is key, because they are the prospective planned givers who possess enough assets to make significant planned gifts. Since people use earnings and accumulated property to provide the necessities and luxuries enjoyed throughout life, owning property assures their economic well-being, as well as that of their families and perhaps others.

Those who make major current and/or deferred planned gifts will give property what they either consider "overflow"— excess assets or income that can be used to fund major gifts made during a person's life, or "leftover"—which can be used for funding major gifts made at death (e.g., a gift via one's will). All charitable gifts are funded with property in one form or another.

### An Explanation of Property's Place

In 1953, while attending the Institute of Life Insurance Marketing at Southern Methodist University, I heard a story that has been helpful to me in understanding property and how it is used to fund planned gifts.

Centuries ago, an elder was walking in the commons with his son teaching him about tribal customs. They noticed that two men were carrying a severely wounded tribesman on a stretcher toward a funeral pyre.

When asked by the young man what was happening, the father responded by explaining how the tribe dealt with various problems. The father told his son that when a tribesman was injured to the extent that he is unable to hunt, fish, grow food, and care for himself, the tribe's solution is to take the injured one and place him on a funeral pyre. The young tribesman said, "Father, this shouldn't be."

Later that day they watched a woman with two children walking toward the pyre. Afterward, an elderly, hobbling couple made the trek. The son inquired of his father each time about what was happening and received basically the same answer. The woman was a widow, unable to take care of her family. The elderly couple could no longer be independent. Both times the young man said, "Father, this shouldn't be."

The young man thought long and hard about the way the tribe dealt with their own families. He devised a proposal to present to the tribal leaders. The young man suggested that all hunters and farmers set aside a small part of the food they produced. When tribesmen were unable to hunt, fish, and raise food, there would be a reserve from which families could receive help. The disabled, the elderly, those who have emergencies, and the survivors of tribe members could all benefit.

This story illustrates how financial security evolves from property ownership. Without property, which is our accumulated assets, we would be unable to provide for ourselves when we have *emergencies*, when we are *disabled* for a long period of time, when we *die* leaving dependents, and when we *retire*.

## THE CHANGING VALUE OF PROPERTY

Property is referred to as assets, possessions, belongings, holdings, and in many other ways. It can be disposed of through sale or gift to any person(s) or any institution of the owner's choosing.

Generally planned gifts are funded with accumulated assets, which is property—property the owner purchased, discovered, or received as a gift—rather than with earned income. It is important to understand that people often have emotional attachments to the property they own. For example, the family home, farm, ranch, stock in a family business, and other assets may, in the minds of some people, be "sacred" property. Consequently, people tend not to use certain properties to fund charitable gifts unless those gifts are made in memory of parents, a spouse, or others close to the property owner.

The *cost basis* is the value of the property as of the time it is acquired. The *fair market value* at any time after its acquisition is what a willing buyer will pay a willing seller with neither being under compulsion to sell or buy.

The difference between what that accumulated property is worth now as opposed to its original cost, referred to as *capital gains*, can be great. Many older people have owned assets for many years and are (at least on paper) wealthier than they ever dreamed. I recently worked with an 85-year-old, for example, who told me that at age 65, he was worth only $350,000. That $350,000 had grown to $1.5 million, and the owner had done nothing but retire and spend! As a result, this person can make large gifts, if so moved. Rather than give cash, careful givers can fund their major current and deferred planned gifts with property that has increased in value. When people who are giving property have owned it long enough, under tax laws, they may be able to avoid capital gains tax and deduct the fair market value of the property. (Readers should check with tax counsel.)

It is important to understand the "time value" of money when major gifts are being considered. The concept is well known to many givers and should be known to all gift planners and institutional leaders. Take the Rule of 72, for example. By dividing the rate of interest being considered into 72, one can learn the number of years it will take for an asset to double in value. The value of property today is different from what it will be years from now. Recently, Terry Smith, J.D., told a National Planned Giving Institute panel at the College of William and Mary about the importance of time value. He gave this example: "At age 20, Barbara starts to deposit $1000 a year, which she does for 10 years (a total of $10,000) at 7 percent interest. At age 30 she stops making deposits, but leaves the account at interest. Sam, the same age as Barbara, does not begin saving until age 30, but then deposits $1000 per year for the next 35 years (a total of $35,000), also at 7 percent interest. When Barbara and Sam are age 65, Barbara's account will exceed Sam's by more than $9,000 (147,512.45 versus $138,236.88)." Because planned giving includes deferred giving, time value is important.

## REAL VERSUS PERSONAL PROPERTY

Sometimes confusion arises about what is and what is not real and personal property. Land and attachments to the land are referred to as *real property*. Personal property is everything else a person owns. For example, grapevines are considered real property but harvested grapes are personal property. Raisins and juice from the grapes are also personal property.

## TANGIBLE VERSUS INTANGIBLE PROPERTY

People own tangible and intangible property. Automobiles and wristwatches are examples of tangible property; securities, life insurance, leases, and other contractual assets are examples of intangible properties.

## LIFE INTEREST VERSUS REMAINDER INTEREST

Property, whether tangible or intangible, is divided into two parts: the life interest and the remainder interest. (See Exhibit 1.1.) The life interest is the right to use property, such as living in a house for life or receiving the income earned on the property for life. The remainder interest is what is left at the death of the owner. When the owner(s) have the right to the life interest and the remainder interest at the same time, the owner(s) possess the full value of the property. The present value of the life income and/or remainder interest is influenced by the age of the owner(s), the assumed interest rate at the time of the transfer, and the marketability of the property. People may own either interest and may transfer either interest as gifts.

The life interest declines in value while the remainder in-

## Exhibit 1.1   Remainder Interest versus Life Interest

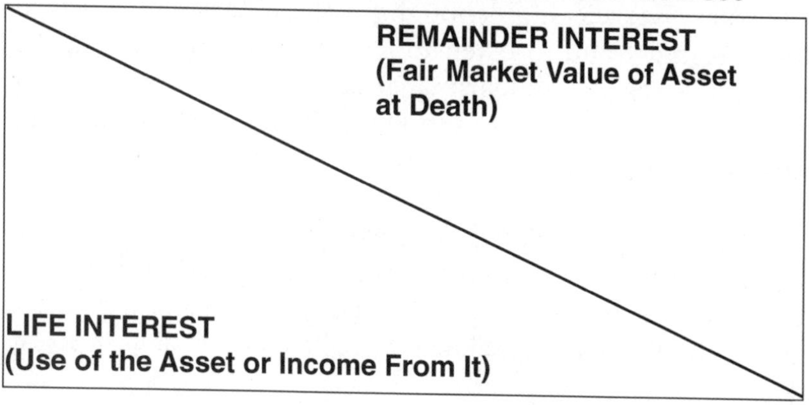

REMAINDER INTEREST
(Fair Market Value of Asset at Death)

LIFE INTEREST
(Use of the Asset or Income From It)

terest increases. The present value of the remainder interest can be estimated mathematically; however, the true value to the recipient will be determined at the time the actual transfer takes place.

## THE GIVER'S CONNECTION TO THE GIFT

As previously mentioned, property, both real and personal, sometimes may have great emotional value to its owner. In some cases, property owners may want to give a particular asset to a charitable institution; in other situations they would not consider giving that property under any circumstances. Charitable gift planners need an awareness of what prospective planned givers think and feel about the property they own.

Since 1959 I have been talking with people about their property. The first important lesson I learned was that I had to earn the right to talk with them about their property. As a charitable gift planner, I was involved with these prospective givers because of the confidence and trust they had in the leadership of the institution for which I worked. I was dependent on these leaders to open doors to the people who would become qualified prospective planned givers. Once the trust level was high enough for them to trust me, I next learned that I had to listen to gain their confidence. In the process, I was able to learn what people would consider giving and what they wanted to keep. Then I could help them give whatever they want to give to the institution(s) of their choice.

Because accumulated property can be so important to those who give and can form some of the largest gifts, the interests of the giver must be the highest concern of the charitable gift planner. The charitable gift planner always must advise the giver to consult with legal or other counsel prior to completing the transfer of property.

Accumulated property can help ensure a secure financial future for a person, a person's family, and the society of which they are a part. That property also can be given through a charitable organization to ensure the future of other people.

# 2 ▼ Current Planned Gifts

## INTRODUCTION

Much of the emphasis on planned giving centers on deferred gift plans that are completed now to be delivered at some point in the future, often at the giver's death.

Current (outright) gifts of assets, as we shall see, are as much planned gifts as are deferred gifts. In addition to the personal satisfaction that comes with making gifts during a lifetime, often tax benefits come with such gifts. Cash and other property such as land, patents, royalties, farm animals, and collections can be excellent gifts. Other outright gifts may consist of securities, income from charitable lead trusts, gifts of cash value and dividends from life insurance and annuity policies, withdrawals from retirement plans, deeds to real estate, and any other personal or real property.

Let's look at some examples of people who have made major current planned gifts.

A farmer wanted to give part of his wheat crop to his church but couldn't take this gift to the church. He loaded his truck with wheat and drove it to the church, stopped, gave it symbolically, then delivered the wheat to the grain elevator, weighed and sold it, and got a receipt which he gave to the church. The church could later redeem the receipt for cash.

- Physicians and dentists provide health care and dental service to youths living in children's homes and to the poor.
- A business executive may give a 99-year lease with 75 years to completion to a university.
- A real estate investor gives land contracts, mortgages, leases, notes, and other contractual arrangement to her alma mater.
- A rancher discovers oil on his land and assigns royalties to four charitable institutions.
- An author gives royalties from published writings to an overseas missionary organization.

The following sections examine specific current gifts often made to charitable institutions.

## GIFTS OF SECURITIES

There are three ways to give stocks and bonds, including mutual funds. People can:

1. Give a security outright worth more now than what they originally paid for it.
2. Sell a security to a charitable institution at a reduced price.
3. Sell a security that is worth less than when they bought it and give the proceeds to the organization.

### Gifts of Securities with Higher Value

When marketable securities—stocks, mutual funds, bonds— and other assets that have increased in value over a period of years are given to qualified charitable institutions, some donors can receive federal income-, gift-, and estate-tax benefits, which includes avoiding the payment of capital gains taxes. For example, Mr. and Mrs. Adams, 62 and 64, have been long-term regular donors to the local symphony orchestra. They decided to send a check for $10,000. Upon receipt of the check, the director called to thank them for the gift. He told them that it was management policy to offer assistance to anyone making a gift of such an amount by helping them determine whether there were ways to give more efficiently, decrease their cost of making the gift, or to help increase the amount of the gift without increasing its cost. Mr. and Mrs. Adams revealed that they owned securities that had increased in value since they were acquired a number of years ago. Some of their securities had more than doubled in value—in fact, the increase was 400 percent and more. When they realized how they could increase the amount of their gift at no greater out-of-pocket cost, they gave 100 shares of XYZ stock that had a fair market value of more than $12,000. Mr. and Mrs. Adams had been unaware of the advantages of giving appreciated assets rather than cash. The Adamses were able to take a larger deduction on their income-tax return and avoid the capital-gains tax, and the symphony received a larger gift.

## Bargain Sale Gifts

Another kind of current planned gift used by those who own appreciated securities is the bargain-sale gift transaction between a giver and a charity. If Mr. and Mrs. Ellis owned a stock with a fair market value of $25,000 that originally cost $13,000, they could sell the stock to the community hospital at a bargain price of $13,000. When the hospital accepted the offer, it would pay Mr. and Mrs. Ellis $13,000 for the security.

The couple has, in effect, given the increase in value and kept their original investment. Tax counsel must be consulted to determine the tax benefits available to Mr. and Mrs. Ellis.

## Gifts of Securities that Have Depreciated in Value

If stocks have decreased or gone down in value since they were purchased, usually it is best for givers to sell the stocks first and claim a capital loss on the federal income-tax return. Then the proceeds from the sale of the stocks can be given as a contribution to a charitable institution. The federal income-tax deduction will be for the amount of the gift, which is equal to the proceeds from the sale of the stocks.

For example, Jane Little wanted to give $10,000 to her church. She had read that it would be to her advantage to give stocks instead of cash. Without knowing anything about the stock she owned, she selected 100 shares of stock that had declined in value. She had paid $22,000 for the stock and its present value was just $10,000. Since that was the amount she wanted to give, she mailed the stock certificate to her church. It was accepted and acknowledged, no questions asked.

What Ms. Little did not know was that she could have made the gift at less cost by selling the stock herself and giving the proceeds to the church. In this way she may have been able to take a capital loss on her federal income-tax return and then deducted the proceeds that she gave away. By acting without counsel, Ms. Little gave unwisely.

## Transferring Securities to a Charitable Institution

People can transfer securities to charitable institutions in the following ways.

- Ask their broker to transfer the stock certificate to the charitable institution by putting the institution's name on the certificate. (Exhibit 2.1 provides a sample assignment form.)
- Complete the back of the stock certificate and sign their name(s) exactly as it appears on the face of the certificate. A stockbroker or a bank officer must guarantee the signature.
- Send the unsigned stock certificate in one envelope and a "Form Separate from Stock Certificate," commonly known as a "stock power," in another envelope. The form

---

**Exhibit 2.1  Sample Stock Transfer Assignment Form**

*Sample assignment form, used in transferring securities.*

ASSIGNMENT SEPARATE FROM CERTIFICATE
For Value Received, _____
hereby sell, assign, and transfer unto _____

_____  (____) Shares of the _____
Capital Stock of the _____
standing in _____ name of the books of said
_____ represented by Certificate No. _____
herewith and do hereby irrevocably constitute and appoint
_____ attorney to transfer
the said stock on the books of the within named Company with full power of substitution in the premises.
Dated _____
IN THE PRESENCE OF                   X_____
_____      X_____
                                     Signature guaranteed

                                     _____
                                     (Your signature must be guaranteed
                                     by your broker or banker.)

must be signed, and a bank officer or a stockbroker must guarantee the signature.

The best way for prospective givers to transfer securities is to write to the holder of the securities and ask for instructions. Use Exhibit 2.2 to conduct a personal securities inventory.

## OTHER POSSESSIONS

In addition to cash, it is very common to give other possessions to nonprofit institutions. In the past this often took the form of crops and farm animals. Today it can be anything from heirlooms to intellectual property, paintings, patents, and the like.

Antiques, jewelry, and collections are very common and popular gifts to charitable institutions, and people generally can deduct the fair market value if they give them to a qualified charity. One word of caution, however: Many givers are disappointed when institutions receive only what they view as a small percentage of the gift's fair market value. To avoid this, givers should be encouraged to have their valuables appraised and get a written appraisal for each item, and then decide if it is better to sell the items and give the proceeds or give the items themselves to the charity. It is essential to have competent counsel to advise on unusual gifts of possessions.

For example, Mr. and Mrs. Rhodes have a painting that has a fair market value of $10,000 and that cost them $5,000 at the time of purchase. They explore the different options that are available to them: If they give it to a museum for display, they may deduct the full $10,000 fair market value of the painting; however, if the painting is given to a hospital or another unrelated institution, the same deduction rules may not apply. It is important for them to check with competent

## Exhibit 2.2  How to Transfer Securities

**1. Complete the following securities inventory.**
**Personal Securities Inventory**

| Number of Shares of Stock or Amount of Bonds | Kinds of Securities | Original Cost | Present Fair Market Value | Amount of Increase in Value | Amount of Decrease in Value |
|---|---|---|---|---|---|
| $_____ | Common stocks | $_____ | $_____ | $_____ | $_____ |
| $_____ | Preferred stock | $_____ | $_____ | $_____ | $_____ |
| $_____ | Corporation bonds | $_____ | $_____ | $_____ | $_____ |
| $_____ | Notes receivable | $_____ | $_____ | $_____ | $_____ |
| $_____ | U.S. Government Savings Bonds | $_____ | $_____ | $_____ | $_____ |
| $_____ | U.S. Government or Government agency bonds | $_____ | $_____ | $_____ | $_____ |

| | | | |
|---|---|---|---|
| Tax-exempt municipal bonds | $_____ | $_____ | $_____ |
| Other bonds | $_____ | $_____ | $_____ |
| Certificates of deposit, banks, savings & loans, & loan association | $_____ | $_____ | $_____ |
| Leases, mortgages, land contracts | $_____ | $_____ | $_____ |
| Other | $_____ | $_____ | $_____ |

If you plan to give securities to any charitable institution, review your security holding with that institution's planned giving officer and/or financial advisor.

Here are four ways to transfer securities to charities:

1. Ask your stockbroker to transfer the stock certificates to the institution. (Contact the institution for the correct name.) OR

2. Complete the back of the stock certificate and sign your name exactly as it appears on the face of the certificate. It will be necessary for your signature to be guaranteed by a stockbroker or your bank officer.

OR

3. You send the institution the unsigned stock certificate in one envelope and a "Form Separate from Stock Certificate," commonly known as a "stock power," in another envelope. You must sign the form and have your bank signature guaranteed by a stockbroker or bank officer.

OR

4. You e-mail, write, or call the stock transfer agent for advice on transferring stock to a charitable institution.

tax counsel before deciding what the deduction will be and if an appraisal will be needed.

Mr. and Mrs. McElroy owned some antique jewelry and a valuable coin collection. Mrs. McElroy served on the board of a retirement center and was considering giving the institution a collection of coins and jewelry. She first had each item appraised by an expert and obtained a written appraisal of each item. She then delivered the items to the retirement home and asked for a receipt describing the items, without any dollar amount given. She was able to establish an income-tax deduction equal to the fair market value of the items given. A bona fide appraisal helped substantiate the income-tax deduction taken for such a contribution. One caution: Institutions should not place a value on gifts of property. It is the responsibility of givers to arrive at the value that is used for tax purposes. The institutional leadership may feel free to ask for copies of any appraisals after the fact to help them place a value on the gift for their purposes.

## ANNUAL GIFTS OF INCOME FROM CHARITABLE LEAD TRUSTS

A charitable lead trust arrangement permits the giver to designate regular annual or more frequent gifts of income from the trust to charitable institutions. At the end of the selected term of years or at the death of the giver/trustor, the principal of the trust reverts to the giver/trustor or to designated beneficiaries, probably children or other family members, but possibly charitable institutions.

If Mr. and Mrs. DeMere wanted to provide support for the ballet for a certain term of years or for the rest of their lives, they might consider using a charitable lead trust. They could transfer $1,000,000 to a trustee and provide that 6 percent (or some selected percentage) of the initial net fair market value of the trust assets be paid by the trustee to the ballet. The trust would continue for as long as either of them lived. Upon the death of the survivor, the trust assets would revert to their children, as the DeMeres wished. The trustee would make the fixed annual payments to the ballet, and at the termination of the trust, the children would receive the assets. This gift arrangement is an important consideration for people who have estates that are large enough to place them in higher federal income-, gift-, and estate-tax brackets.

## GIFTS OF EXISTING LIFE INSURANCE

People can make planned gifts by the assignment of annual dividends paid on their life insurance policies or make outright gifts of policies that may have served their purposes. This is sometimes the ideal source of funds to make current gifts. As the donor's children mature, family protection may no longer be needed. When the mortgage is paid off, mortgage insurance is no longer needed. When a business interest is sold, life insurance held for business reasons no longer needs to be held. If assets have been accumulated for retirement, life insurance may not be needed. Life insurance protection that was purchased to protect a beneficiary who predeceased the policyholder in death sometimes makes an ideal gift. These "used " life insurance policies help guarantee money needed for education, medical aid, and shelter, and if not used for these purposes, they can bring satisfaction to motivated givers.

For example, suppose Mr. and Mrs. Bailey had a $100,000 ordinary life insurance policy on which they were paying annual premiums of $3,500 a year. The policy originally had been purchased to provide money for the education of their daughter; however, she died prematurely and the life insurance policy was never used for that purpose. She was a musician who loved the symphony, and Mr. and Mrs. Bailey decided to transfer the ownership of the policy to the symphony as an outright gift to establish a memorial to their daughter. While their primary motivation was to provide support for the organization, certain tax benefits also come with this kind of transfer. The symphony may surrender the policy for its cash surrender value and dividends, or the policy could be continued in force and paid for by the symphony or by Mr. and Mrs. Bailey, who could take certain tax deductions. Advice of tax counsel should be sought.

## GIFTS OF REAL ESTATE

Commercial real estate, such as apartments, buildings, or a private home can be given outright to a charitable organization. The giver usually will receive a federal income-tax deduction for the present fair market value, thus saving capital-gains tax. Tax counsel can provide other details. For example, David Franklin, 68, had been a farmer for most of his life. The income from his savings and rental property would provide adequate retirement income. Over the years he had given to several religious institutions, and he decided to deed the rental property to one specific organization. He did so, and the organization later sold the property for $110,000. Franklin's original cost was less than $25,000. By giving the property, he saved the capital-gains tax and was allowed to deduct the entire fair market value of the property on his tax return. Since $110,000 was more than he was permitted to deduct in the year he made the gift, he was allowed to deduct the excess during the next few tax years, up to a maximum. Had he sold the property himself, he would have paid thousands of dollars in capital-gains taxes on the $85,000 increase in value.

However, if property has a present fair market value

less than the original cost, givers should consider selling it themselves, giving the proceeds to the organizations, and deducting the capital loss from their taxes. For example, Tom and Carla Smith bought some resort property several years ago for $75,000. A prospective buyer has offered to purchase it for $60,000. If they sell it for that amount, they will experience a $15,000 loss. If they want to contribute $60,000 to charity, they can give the proceeds from the sale.

Whenever real estate is used to fund a current or deferred planned gift, special attention should be given to environmental and other concerns. (Advice of counsel should be sought on all transfers of real estate.)

## GIFTS FROM RETIREMENT ACCOUNTS

Gifts from Individual Retirement Accounts (IRAs), 401(k) plans, and other pension and profit-sharing plans can be withdrawn without penalty and given by people who continue working and earning after reaching age 59½. Withdrawals will have to be reported as income for tax purposes.

Suppose Mr. Fuller has rollover IRAs in which he deposited all of his qualified retirement assets. Mr. Fuller continues to work and earn money, and he also has securities and notes. Let's say he wants to make a special gift to expand the memorial already established in the name of his mother. He could add to this memorial by making several annual withdrawals from his retirement plan between ages 59½ and 70½. He must report what is withdrawn from the retirement account as income but may deduct what is given to the memorial fund for his mother. However, instead of giving the money he took from his retirement account each year, he could give appreciated mutual funds or other stocks from other accounts he has and realize other important tax benefits. If the retirement fund investment earns an average of 10 percent annually, and he decides to give the earnings each year, he will have what he started with originally, even after making these withdrawals. Making these kinds of gifts offers a number of important tax considerations, and tax counsel is essential.

## CREATIVE ARRANGEMENTS BY CORPORATIONS

Sometimes corporations make current planned gifts. Some corporate sponsorships are carefully planned because companies want their money to be as productive as possible for the company. In a real sense, corporations do not give because something is received in return. While corporations are not created in order to give, they may, through sponsorships, receive help in meeting their marketing objectives while positioning themselves as good corporate citizens. Support they give to carefully selected charitable institutions in the form of planned corporate sponsorships can be of great help to the community. Corporate funding is included here because most financial development executives, especially in small to medium-size institutions, often have a broad job description that includes securing sponsorships from corporations as well as gifts from individuals.

Real-life example: Three years ago I was serving as a member of the board of trustees of the Memphis Museums, Inc. One million dollars was needed quickly to open an IMAX theater at the Pink Palace Museum. A successful capital campaign had just been completed, and we didn't want to announce another campaign to secure this money. It appeared that we wouldn't need outright gifts because it was possible the projected income from the IMAX theater would service the debt. We considered borrowing, but what we needed was a corporate partner that would join with us to accomplish something good for the community and for the corporation.

The Union Planters National Bank of Memphis decided to lend us $1,000,000, interest subsidized, for ten years. The loan was to be repaid to the bank in eight years, but the museum could wait two years before beginning the payments. After nearly three years, we have an ongoing, successful Union Planters IMAX Theater operation.

This is quid pro quo at its best; the museum received the IMAX theater without capital expenditures and the bank got its name and logo on all publicity, promotions, and advertising. Hundreds of thousands of impressions are made, and the facility served over 290,000 visitors in its second full year of operation. Many people are being drawn to the museum for family entertainment and education because of the Union Planters IMAX Theater. People who probably would have never visited the museum are enjoying planetarium shows and exhibits. Bank and museum leadership feel positive about the planned gift/sponsorship partnership. The additional benefit of this arrangement was a quiet campaign to capitalize the start-up costs of the theater, which produced $500,000 additional revenue to underwrite staffing, marketing, and unplanned theater enhancements.

Charitable institutions can obtain corporate sponsorships when they have a big idea that serves the customer base and stockholders of a corporation as well as the constituencies of the charitable institution. When a corporation has creative leaders, such as the management and directors of Union Planters National Bank, who want to give back to the community, there is a real opportunity to get together and do something truly creative that serves all parties. Some charitable institutions will need funds to pay for new programs or facilities. The keys to using interest-subsidized loans are these: (1) the program has the potential for producing enough income to pay or service the debt, and (2) the corporation lending the money receives recognition or other public relations benefits. Each situation needs to be researched carefully by counsel representing the charitable institution and corporation. This idea may help others develop a corporate sponsorship that turns into a partnership that serves all parties.

## CONCLUSION

Current planned gifts are increasingly important to the future well-being of charitable institutions. Institutional leaders always need to search for corporations and individuals with a keen interest in the future financial well-being of their institutions.

# 3 ▼ Deferred Planned Gifts

Charitable institutions receive deferred planned gifts when they are designated as beneficiaries in wills, trusts, contracts, or other agreements at the end of a specified term of years or at the death of the giver(s) and/or other designated beneficiary(ies). Sometimes those making deferred planned gift arrangements reserve to themselves the right to receive specified income for a term of years or for the life (or lives) of the named beneficiary. The following deferred planned gift arrangements can be used to transfer remainders from trusts and residues from wills to charities at death.

## THE LAST WILL AND TESTAMENT

A will is the last statement (testament) a person makes to instruct society on what is to happen to the assets that he or she has accumulated during life. The will is the best-known and most widely used estate-transfer document for delivering deferred gifts to charitable institutions at death. Many reports and studies indicate that most charitable institutions receive two-thirds or more of all deferred gift dollars from wills.

THE PLANNED GIFT

A charity can be first, second, or last beneficiary of a will to receive part or all of the proceeds. Most institutions that have been receiving bequests for a long time prefer to be named as the beneficiary to receive part or all of the residue; they know that the average gift from the residue far exceeds the average gift of a specific amount. Some institutions receive as much as 90 percent of their bequest income by being named as the beneficiary for part or all of the residue.

Frances Kelley, 79, knew she needed to update her will, which had not been done since her husband had died. As she looked back on her life, she began thinking of leaving something to her alma mater and to her church. She also wanted to care for her sister and her niece. After considering her options carefully, she decided to make a will leaving stock valued at $60,000 to her sister, her home valued at $80,000 to her niece, $10,000 to her church, and whatever was left at death to her college. By using a simple will, she was able to retain the use of her assets during her lifetime and carry out other giving objectives at her death.

## REVOCABLE LIVING TRUSTS

Revocable living trusts allow prospective planned givers to appoint trustees to receive assets to invest, reinvest, manage, distribute, and even make charitable gifts during life or after death. Living trusts meet people's need for management services while they live, and for family and charitable beneficiaries following death. Trustees are bound by the provisions of the trust itself and by applicable governing laws.

The revocable living trust is being used increasingly for making charitable gifts at death. It has been referred to as the queen of all deferred-giving plans because of its flexibility. People can change their minds and have the trust assets returned to them. Any person or institution may be named as the beneficiary of income and/or principal. The income that can be paid to the giver or charity during life may be fixed or variable, or the income may be accumulated. The trust assets are invested by a trustee, and the giver chooses the beneficiary who receives the income each year. This recipient can be the donor, another person, or an institution.

Very often current planned givers—especially older people—do not make major deferred gifts because they don't want to create irrevocable gift arrangements. Prospective planned givers may need the security of knowing that their assets are available to them during their lifetime for emergencies or when they live longer than expected. Or they simply may want to be free to change their minds. People who want to provide for themselves, for their dependents, and for others and to enhance their own security establish revocable living trusts. The fact that they can have their assets returned often makes it possible for people to give more than they originally thought. Just being able to think "I can get my assets back if I need them" provides needed security for many people and causes them to be more generous.

Charitable gift planners who understand the importance of revocable living trusts and promote them widely and wisely will thrive because they are serving the needs of those who give. As an example, Mr. and Mrs. Wentz have a revocable living trust that is funded with almost all of their securities. They could, through a pourover will, have all of their assets not already a part of the trust flow into the trust at death and be distributed in accordance with its provisions. For example, say the local library is named in their wills to receive a bequest. It is likely that the library would not receive a gift designated in their wills, since all assets will be in the trust and trusts generally take precedence over wills. Mr. and Mrs. Wentz will want to seek legal advice when they consider using revocable living trusts in their estate plan to make certain their plans are coordinated.

Institutional leaders want to know the present value of deferred gift arrangements. Determining the value of irrevocable gift arrangements is not much of a problem, and crediting the present value of the charitable remainder interest of trusts and the gift portions of gift annuities is reasonable. However, if the gift is made via a will, through a revocable living trust, by beneficiary designations in a life insurance, annuity policy, retirement plan, or by other revocable contractual arrangements, an institution can count very little unless it has an established pattern of gift income from such gifts over a long period . . . and some institutions do have. My view is to book revocable gifts at $1.00 or some other low figure and save the counting until they mature. While many managers do not favor this method, revocable gift arrangements *can* be changed. Although most matured deferred gifts are received from revocable gift arrangements, I believe most of these gift decisions are made after the donor(s) reached age 70. It is very difficult for management to accurately predict values of revocable giving arrangements of any kind without the benefit of a long history of receiving many of these gifts.

## LIFE ESTATE AGREEMENTS

Through the use of a life estate agreement, a person can deed a home or a family farm to a charitable institution and reserve the right to continue living in or on it and using it for life. On the giver's death, the charity becomes the owner of the real estate. This kind of gift may yield federal income-, gift-, and estate-tax savings.

For example, Mr. and Mrs. Sawtell entered into an irrevocable agreement to deed their home situated near the local nature center on the condition that they would be able to continue living there for as long as either of them lived. They

would continue to pay all taxes, insurance, and other mainte-
nance costs and would receive any income the property produced. The couple received favorable federal income-tax
considerations at the time of the gift and possibly other tax
benefits. State and federal laws should be checked with a
competent advisor.

Revocable life estate agreements also can be entered into
between charitable institutions and an individual with a provision added that permits the person to revoke the agreements at any time. There are no tax benefits during the
person's life for making such a gift because the agreement is
revocable. The giver retains the freedom to have it deeded
back to him or her.

While gifts through life estate agreements can be valuable, charitable institutions need to examine carefully the
present and past uses of the property before accepting it;
possible environmental contamination, subsequent cleanup,
or other concerns prove costly to the development and disposition of the real estate.

## EXISTING LIFE INSURANCE AND ANNUITY POLICIES

As mentioned before, life insurance and annuity policies can
be given outright. Policyowners also can direct in the policies
they already own that the proceeds be given to a charitable
institution as a deferred planned gift. This can be done without using a will or a trust. With approximately 400,000,000
life insurance and annuity policies in force insuring the lives
of most Americans, the potential for helping fund charitable
institutions using existing policies is staggering. According to
the 1996 edition of *The Life Insurance Fact Book*, the face
value of these policies exceeded $12 trillion.

The purchase of new life insurance policies may be important to some donors who want to guarantee a long-term pledge. Younger individuals may make annual gifts to be used to purchase life insurance to create a large gift at death.

For example, suppose Dr. Albertson, 37, was provided with a medical education by an uncle and aunt, now deceased. She wants to establish a named memorial for them at the medical school she attended. She is willing to set aside $20,000 annually to create this memorial. Dr. Albertson discussed the idea with a charitable gift planner employed by the medical school, who suggested she might consider purchasing life insurance. Her life underwriter was called, and Dr. Albertson learned that she could give $20,000 annually to the medical school to be used to purchase $1,000,000 of life insurance on her life, which, at her death, would be used to establish a memorial in the names of her uncle and aunt at the medical school. The annual gifts of $20,000 could be deducted as charitable gifts. The policy may be paid up in a shorter period of time by accumulating policy dividends or by the company crediting excess interest earned, if any. The objective is to guarantee the funding of the memorial endowment. At Dr. Albertson's death, the life insurance proceeds will be used to establish a distinguished professorship in the names of her relatives. Legal counsel is advised for Dr. Albertson.

Here is another example. Mr. and Mrs. Schrader, 67 and 65, have policies with $20,000 of cash value available, which will pay them an annuity beginning at age 65. The payment is about $135 per month for as long as either of them lives. If they should die after two years—after receiving only $3,240—the company retains the balance of at least $16,760. However, they could choose to receive smaller annual payments that would guarantee to pay them an annuity for life, but not less than the $20,000. The monthly payments will be slightly less than the $135 mentioned, but if both of the Schraders die before the entire $20,000 has been paid to them, the balance could be directed to the charitable institution of their choice in the form of monthly payments or in a lump sum.

Not all donors know that they can name charitable institutions as the first, second, or last beneficiary for part or all of the proceeds from existing life insurance policies. Such donors should be advised that they can add an institution's name as a beneficiary simply by requesting a change-in-beneficiary form from their life insurance company. Exhibit 3.1 is a sample letter a donor can send to an insurance company. Rarely do life insurance companies encourage policyholders to make charitable gifts by changing beneficiaries on their existing policies. Policy owners have the right to change their beneficiaries on their life insurance and annuity policies, and companies desiring to serve their policyholders are glad to honor requests to change beneficiaries. Donors receive tax benefits when giving old or new policies. Gift planners should check with counsel for specific gift situations.

Unfortunately, charitable institutions have failed to maximize the gift potential of life insurance and annuity policies by not advising prospective planned givers that they can make gifts from existing policies. The emphasis has been on life insurance products, referred to as wealth replacement policies, that are placed on the lives of a couple using a last-to-die policy form naming surviving children as beneficiaries. Life insurance policies were widely promoted during the 1980s and early 1990s by agents and some planned giving executives to make a gift appear to cost the donor or normal survivors little or nothing. Yet the easiest and simplest life insurance gifts are likely to be made by adding a charitable institution's name as the first, second, or last beneficiary in policies already owned. In fact, the longer life insurance policies have been in force, the better they are as charitable gifts because the policies will have built up important cash values, and policies that are no

## Exhibit 3.1   Sample Letter to Life Insurance Companies

Name of Insurance Company
Street
City, State Zip

Refer to policy #_____
Please send me necessary papers to make a charitable gift of life insurance benefits to (name of charitable organization or institution), a not-for-profit corporation. Send the following:

___ I would like to assign my policy dividends.

___ I would like to name (organization or institution) as:
   ___ Primary beneficiary
   ___ Secondary beneficiary
   ___ Final beneficiary
   ___ For a percent of proceeds

___ I would like to transfer policy ownership to (organization or institution) as the irrevocable owner and beneficiary.

___ I would like to name (organization or institution) as remainder beneficiary in my annuity or supplementary contract should I die before receiving all payments guaranteed.

Signed,

_____
Name of policyholder

longer needed sometimes are given outright during the policy-holder's lifetime. When charitable gift planners consider encouraging gifts of life insurance proceeds, they should seek existing policies. Almost all individuals own one or more policies, and the older the policies are, the better they are as charitable gifts. Since there are more than 400,000,000 life insurance policies now in force: Why plant trees if all you want is fruit?

34

## IRAs AND OTHER RETIREMENT PLANS

Gifts from retirement plans provide some of the greatest deferred-giving opportunities for charitable institutions. Charitable institutions that have donors who have overfunded retirement plans (and many do) may discover major gifts that can be made after the retirees' deaths. The estimated value of the funds in tax-advantaged Individual Retirement Accounts (IRAs) and other retirement plans exceed $5 trillion. More than 100,000,000 Americans are eligible to participate in these tax-favored retirement plans. Consequently, the leaders of charitable institutions who want to build future income must emphasize the importance of gifts of retirement property.

The simplest and possibly the best deferred gift arrangement for retirement property is for the charity to be named as the first, second, or last beneficiary for part or all of the proceeds left in the fund at the death of an individual and/or surviving spouse. (See Exhibit 3.2.) More than likely, most gifts from retirement plans will bypass state probate and will be delivered to the charity quickly and efficiently through the retirement plan document itself. Many people discover that their retirement assets are not "tax friendly" when left to their children or beneficiaries other than spouses. Retirement property is probably the best gift that can be made to charities after the death of both spouses and very likely it is the least desirable gift to leave to children. In other words, it will cost donors less to give charities retirement assets than to give them to children. Deferred planned gifts from retirement plans could become one of the two or three most important deferred gift sources to charitable institutions. Making gifts through retirement plans is simpler than making gifts through wills. A written request to the plan administrator may be all that is required. The prospective planned giver needs to contact the administrators of qualified retirement plans for specific instructions.

## Exhibit 3.2   Sample Change-of-Beneficiary Form

*Sample change-of-beneficiary form: To be used for adding charitable or noncharitable beneficiaries. Members should request a form from the financial institution handling their IRA.*

INDIVIDUAL RETIREMENT ACCOUNT
CHANGE OF BENEFICIARY

TO: IRA Section

I hereby revoke any beneficiary designation as previously made with respect to this account and I hereby direct that in the event of my death any balance of my Individual Retirement Account No. _____ be paid in a lump sum payment to:

Primary Beneficiary(ies):

Name: _____   Relationship:_____

Date of Birth:_____

Address: _____
  Street      City      State      Zip Code

Second Beneficiary(ies):

Name: _____   Relationship:_____

Date of Birth:_____

Address:_____
  Street      City      State      Zip Code

I understand this Change of Beneficiary will be effective on the date of receipt by the Custodian.

I retain the right to revoke this designation of beneficiary and to designate a new beneficiary at any time by communicating to the Custodian in writing. I understand that any balance in this account will be includable in my estate for federal estate-tax purposes. If said beneficiary does not survive me or if the Custodian cannot locate said beneficiary after reasonable search, I direct that any balance in this account be paid to _____

_____, a qualified nonprofit institution.
*(Name and Address of Charity)*

Date Executed _____   _____
                                      *Signature of Account Owner*

Witness Signature _____

Witness Address    _____

                   _____

Date received by Custodian _____   By: _____

Mr. and Mrs. Hernandez could make a current planned gift from Mr. Hernandez's retirement plan. He also could use the same retirement plan document to make a deferred planned gift. The plan administrator would supply him with the appropriate form to change beneficiaries, and Mr. Hernandez's instructions would be recorded officially.

Retirement plan property also may be used to fund charitable remainder trusts to provide an annual income for the life of a surviving spouse and also benefit surviving children. Complicated tax considerations should be considered carefully by competent tax counsel before embarking on such a plan. In general, the simplest and very likely the best arrangement for giving retirement property to charity at death is to name the charity as an outright beneficiary at the death of the surviving spouse. There are, of course, exceptions. One caution to charitable institutions being asked to serve as trustee of trusts funded with retirement property is to consider carefully the true costs of management and administration and, more important, to make certain the present value of the charitable remainder interest is adequate to justify assuming this responsibility.

## PRODUCTS FROM FINANCIAL SERVICE INSTITUTIONS AND CREDIT UNIONS

Prospective planned givers may be able to avoid probate by giving money invested in certificates of deposit (CDs) with banks, savings and loan associations, and credit unions, or they may transfer securities from brokerage accounts to charitable institutions at death. The certificates of deposits will include the name of the depositor, followed by the words "in trust for" (ITF) or "paid on death" (POD), followed by the charitable institution's name. A similar arrangement, referred to as transfer on death (TOD), may be available for giving securities from brokerage accounts. (Advisors should check state laws concerning these transfers.)

If Mr. and Mrs. Abrams had invested in certificates of deposit (CD) in their bank, they could request that a retirement center be named to receive the money invested in CDs at the death of the surviving member of the couple. Of course, state laws must be checked to learn of any restrictions in their state of residence.

## GIVING-FOR-INCOME PLANS: OTHER OPTIONS

It is possible for donors to give cash or other property in trust now and receive an income for life. This is a real gift. When donors give in exchange for income, they keep the life interest part and give the remainder interest part. When a charitable organization is the beneficiary named in a giving-for-income trust, the gift the charity receives is known as the charitable remainder interest. Since the beneficiary institution is a qualified charity, donors are entitled to a charitable deduction on their federal income-tax return in the year of the gift.

Three basic irrevocable giving-for-income plans are in widespread use by charitable institutions: the pooled income fund, charitable remainder trusts (annuity trusts and unitrusts), and charitable gift annuities. While these are old concepts, they are relatively new in some respects. These are plans that have proven successful for many donors and charities over a number of years. Each of these plans is distinctive, and each is designed to serve a definite need of the donor.

Charitable institutions sometimes serve as trustee (planners should check applicable state laws) for those making gifts through charitable remainder trusts and pooled income plans, or they may manage the investment accounts that assure the annual payments promised in gift annuity contracts.

It is unwise for trustees and the managements of most charitable institutions to take responsibility for day-to-day investment decisions unless they are experienced and have a
proven record of success managing these kinds of investment. Management must consider carefully what gift
arrangements they will and will not accept. What will the gift
be worth to the institution at the projected death of the
donor? Sometimes givers who are in the "young" and
"young-old" age category, 55 to 70, will ask for higher payouts, which may leave little or nothing for the charity after
the person's death. It is important for institutions to determine, in advance, the minimum present value of the charitable remainder interest that will be acceptable before agreeing
to serve as trustee. In addition, when an institution acts as
trustee, trustee fees should be charged as an expense to the
trust, instead of using other donors' gifts to pay for the cost
of administering these planned gifts.

The institution's plan for the use of the gift may be as important to the giver as the planned gift arrangement itself. As
a general rule, people make gifts because they have an interest in helping fund the vision and mission of an institution,
which has presented its case for giving effectively. Qualified
prospective planned givers want to be a part of something
they believe to be worthwhile. The ways in which they
choose to give depend on their own circumstances. Through
careful planning often they can give more effectively and, as
a result, increase their gifts.

## Pooled Income Funds

Pooled income fund agreements provide for the transfer of
money or other property into a pooled trust that ultimately
will belong to the institution. Donors transfer assets as gifts
that are made a part of a pooled fund out of which the

trustee distributes to the giver a pro rata share of the income earned from the fund's investment. Upon the deaths of those who receive income, their "units" in the pool become gifts to the institution.

For example, Mr. and Mrs. O'Connor, 67 and 70, have a large estate. They transfer $100,000 of highly appreciated stocks to an institutions' pooled income fund. The trust assets are invested so the O'Connors can conservatively expect an annual return of 5 percent, or approximately $5,000, over a long period. They decide they have plenty of income and that the payments should go to Mrs. O'Connor's mother. This provides Mrs. O'Connor's mother with an income that will continue for her lifetime. The gift would be irrevocable, and there are federal income, gift, and estate tax implications to be considered.

## Charitable Remainder Unitrusts

The charitable remainder unitrust is a trust designed to receive a person's assets and make variable lifetime annual payments equal to a percentage of the fair market value of trust assets, determined annually. There are three kinds of charitable remainder unitrusts: (1) the straight unitrust, which pays at least 5 percent of the fair market value of the assets determined annually to the beneficiaries; (2) the net-income-only unitrust, which pays all the income earned up to the amount stated in the trust and must be no more than the stated percentage in any year; and (3) the net-income-plus-makeup unitrust, which provides that when the earnings are higher than the stated percentage amount, the excess will be carried forward and more income can be paid to the beneficiary to make up for any deficiencies in income received in past or future years.

Mr. McBain, 65, owns a farm and wants to make a gift

to a small private college now and receive a life income. The farming operation is netting about $6,000 each year. He would like to increase his income but does not want to pay the large capital-gains tax that would be due if he sold the land himself. He could transfer the farm into a net income charitable remainder unitrust with the college as the charitable remainder beneficiary. The trustee is fortunate enough to sell the farm for $150,000 and reinvest the proceeds. Each year the trustee pays 6.5 percent of the net fair market value of the trust assets, determined annually, to Mr. McBain. The total fair market value of the $150,000 trust at the end of the first year and the first year income is $9750, an increase of $3,750. By using a charitable remainder unitrust, Mr. McBain was able to: (1) make a substantial deferred gift to the college; (2) avoid capital-gains tax; (3) receive an income-tax deduction; and (4) receive an increased life income that also may be eligible for favorable tax treatment each year.

## Charitable Remainder Annuity Trusts

The charitable remainder annuity trust is a trust designed to receive a person's assets subject to the trustee paying fixed annual income for life that is equal to at least 5 percent of the initial net fair market value of trust at the time assets were delivered to the trustee.

For example, Mr. and Mrs. Dortch, ages 74 and 69, own appreciated stocks valued at 20 times the original cost when purchased 10 years ago. They have not received any dividends to date. They want to increase their income for retirement and make a gift when they die. They transfer the stock into a charitable remainder annuity trust to pay 7 percent of the initial net fair market value of the stock annually. By so doing they are able to: (1) make a gift to charity at death; (2) avoid capital-gains tax now; (3) receive an income-tax deduction now for the present value of the charitable remainder interest; and (4) exchange a non–income-producing asset for a fixed percentage annual income for the life of both of them.

## CHARITABLE GIFT ANNUITIES

Charitable gift annuities are giving plans that appeal to many who cannot give in amounts large enough to warrant a separate trust. Charitable gift annuities make fixed annual payments of principal and interest for life to whomever the giver names (self and/or another). Charitable gift annuities are designed to make the promised annual payments for life of the annuitant(s); and to provide, on average, at least 50 percent (the residuum) of the original gift to be used by the charity at the donor's death. The gift to the charitable institution at death is what makes charitable gift annuities different from commercial annuities. The annual payment from charitable gift annuities should always be lower than what would be received from commercial annuities. What makes charitable gift annuities worthwhile to donors is the value that the givers place on giving and the annual payments they receive. Many charities do not offer opportunities to give through charitable gift annuities.

## FUNDING CHARITABLE GIVING PLANS THROUGH WILLS

Emma Mays, age 74, has been volunteering and giving to a social service agency for years. She would like to pass something on to the agency in her will. She also has a brother for whom she wants to provide an income for life.

Ms. Mays consulted with her lawyer and asked, "How can I provide for my brother if he survives me and also give to the social service agency?"

There are four plans you can use. She can instruct the executor of her estate to transfer funds to the institution conditioned on her brother receiving specified annual payments for his life. The payments would be based on her brother's attained age at her death. At her brother's death, anything left goes to the agency. This arrangement is referred to as a *testamentary survivorship gift annuity*. Another method is to instruct the executor of her estate to create a *charitable remainder annuity* trust, which will pay her brother a fixed income for life, or to establish a *charitable remainder unitrust*, which would pay her brother a variable income for life. To qualify for federal tax benefits with either of these trust plans, the minimum annual payment to Ms. Mays's brother must be at least 5 percent of the initial net fair market value of the annuity trust or 5 percent of the fair market value of the trust assets, determined annually, if the unitrust is used. If the social service agency has a *pooled income plan*, Ms. Mays can designate her money to that fund, and her brother would receive his pro-rata share of the income earned by the fund each year.

In any of these plans, whatever remains at the death of Ms. Mays's brother becomes the property of the social service agency.

If Ms. Mays selects one of the two available charitable remainder trusts, the trustee can be directed to pay trust income. Suppose the amount of annual income in either of the charitable remainder trusts is 7.5 percent. The annual income would be $7,500 or 7.5 percent of the initial net fair market value a year for the life of the brother, if the annuity trust is elected. It would be 7.5 percent of the fair market value of trust assets, determined annually, if the unitrust is used. Whatever remains in the principal of either trust or the pooled income fund at death of the brother goes to the social service agency.

Emotional considerations led Emma Mays to plan for the care of her invalid brother should she predecease him. She went to her attorney expecting to have her will prepared but was able to achieve a better solution. By using one of the plans discussed in the meeting, Ms. Mays was able to make a sound financial plan and a gift without diminishing her own security while living or that of her brother, upon her death.

Such trusts, when established during life, will provide a current federal income-tax deduction to the donor. However, if an estate is small, it might be unwise for a donor to place very much of the assets in an irrevocable contract or trust arrangement during her lifetime.

## OTHER CONTRACTUAL ASSET TRANSFERS

Properties, such as certificates of deposit, life insurance, retirement plans, notes, leases, mortgages, land contracts, royalties, patents, and other personal property where ownership is evidenced by a contract, may be transferred to an individual or charitable institution by assignment at death without using a will or a trust. For example, donors can give by assigning mortgages they own to any institution unless it is prohibited by state law. Planners should check with appropriate counsel.

## CONCLUSION

When people believe that it is wise for them to plan carefully for the future, they will also want to have, as part of their plans, provisions that will help them give more effectively.

Many of these givers want to know about creative ways of giving. Deferred planned gift arrangements may offer advantages for both givers and charitable institutions. One or more of the aforementioned plans of giving could be right for all parties interested in helping fund the future of charitable institutions.

# II ▼ THE PLANNED GIVER

Planned givers receive sheer joy from giving. Only those who make carefully thought out voluntary gifts experience this kind of joy.

Planned givers receive dividends from giving that are much higher than the dividends they receive from other investments. Through their gifts they make it possible for the mentally ill, the physically impaired, and those with spiritual, psychological, financial, and other problems to get the help they need.

Charitable givers can give through planned gift arrangements and receive income for a number of years or even for a lifetime, as discussed in Part I. In Part II, we now examine the traits and motivations of donors who are likely to be prospective planned givers. Satisfying a built-in need to give and showing how to give effectively without adversely affecting economic freedom and financial security is the focus of Part II.

# 4 ▼ Who Makes Planned Gifts?

Who are the people who make planned gifts? This is a fundamental question for institutional management to answer before beginning a new planned giving program or attempting to build upon one already in existence.

## GIVER PROFILE

The people who make deferred planned gifts today are very likely current and former givers who made small regular gifts in the past. They learned to give at home, in church, at school, or from others they met early in life.

Planned givers are more comfortable and generous when they are confident they are giving assets they will not need in the future. While they will give some accumulated assets as outright current gifts, they are likely to give more to fund future deferred planned gifts. They are more apt to give what remains in their estates at death than to give now through irrevocable methods such as charitable remainder trusts.

When working with prospective planned givers, charitable gift planners need to be more concerned about the giver's desires and schedule than the institution's agenda for seeking gifts. Planned giving awareness should be ongoing throughout the life of an institution. More planned gifts will be made over the long term than during a series of periodic campaigns. When charitable institutions build their planned giving programs around people's need to give rather around than the institution's need for money, people will consider making major current or deferred planned gifts when various events occur in their lives. Examples of these events are marriage, births, deaths, divorces, and successes or failures. Another factor in building a planned giving program involves the institution's ability to articulate its vision, its mission, and its case for giving to the prospect. And of course, the most important factor is age.

## AGE MATTERS

If charitable gift planners could choose whether to know their prospect's financial capabilities or the person's age, I would suggest choosing age information. The prospective donor's age is the single most important piece of information charitable gift planners can obtain prior to making the initial contact. Age doesn't tell much about the assets people own except that if they are older, there is a greater possibility that they have had time to acquire more assets than younger people. Age doesn't indicate whether people will consider making planned gifts. It does, however, tell us that they have reached the time in life when motivated people are most likely to discuss making planned gifts, which is especially important when seeking deferred planned gifts. Most current and deferred planned gifts are completed by those who are in the middle or final seasons of life. Those who give tend to respond to institutions that have served them, their families, and their communities in the past.

Some members of every age group make planned gifts.

People make different kinds of gifts at different times in life. All potential planned givers can be grouped into four categories:

- The young—under age 55
- The young-old—age 56 to 70
- The old—71 to 85
- The old-old—over age 85

As life expectancies continue to increase, perhaps there should be a fifth category referred to as the centurions.

## The Young and Young-Old (Under 55 to 70)

The young rarely make deferred planned gifts. Some of the older members in the young-old group do make substantial current planned gifts. When people in this age group have paid for their children's education, retired their home mortgages, and are earning more than ever before, they are capable of making major current planned gifts, but most of them do not give much. The first large gift may be made during these years in the context of a capital campaign.

However, those who are motivated to give, experience joy and satisfaction from giving. Some fear they will need some or all of their assets before they die. As a result of this common fear, many people may decrease or even discontinue making outright gifts as they get older.

Too much emphasis is being put on what Baby Boomers will not give and not enough is being placed on what some of them can and will do. Baby Boomers fall within the young part of this category. Some of those in the young and young-old group may name charitable institutions to receive proceeds at death as the first, second, or last beneficiary in wills, trusts, existing life insurance policies, retirement plans, and other contractual arrangements, but most will delay making this kind of decision until they are older. Those who name charities as beneficiaries probably will change their plans several times prior to death. Studies reveal that most bequests that mature come from wills made after age 70.

I predict the Baby Boomers will continue the family tradition and give much like their parents gave. They will respond to institutions with outstanding missions they believe in in just the same way people born in the 1920s are responding today. When Baby Boomers have confidence in the leadership of charitable institutions they are drawn to, when they have an overflow of assets while they live and likely to have leftovers after they die, and when they are willing to see competent planned giving executives to discuss planned giving, and if they are motivated, a few of them will give just as generously as a few in previous generations gave.

People in the young-old group who have substantial accumulated assets may consider making irrevocable gift arrangements, gifts conditioned on receiving a lifetime income. The plans generally selected are charitable remainder trusts, pooled income funds, deferred-payment gift annuities, life estate contracts, and charitable lead trusts. (The people in this category may benefit from federal income and estate tax benefits.) Zero-coupon bonds, reversionary charitable lead trusts, or life insurance gifts may appeal to donors with significant assets.

## The Old and the Old-Old

Major current giving tends to decline when people are "old," especially when they become a part of the old-old category. Since they don't know what the future holds, they tend to reduce current giving at a time when they have more assets and a greater desire to give. Some are frustrated when they feel they must reduce their giving, a deferred planned gift can be the answer—in fact, it may be the only gift some individuals will consider making.

Committed old and old-old people are the best prospective planned givers, and they are the ones who have made plans after age 70 to leave large sums of money to charitable institutions of all kinds. Most of their planned gifts are made using non-income-tax oriented plans of giving; their wills are the primary source.

## LIFE'S MILESTONES

In considering who makes planned gifts, it is important to determine what causes people to make them. People rarely make decisions on planned gifts, especially deferred ones, solely because an institution needs money. They make planned gifts when they are making their wills or other estate-planning arrangements for other reasons. It is important for charitable gift planners to understand what causes people to make wills and/or estate plans. Often people begin planning because of events occurring in their lives. Changing circumstances cause them to become concerned about personal financial security and economic freedom for themselves and their families. These events often surround marriage, divorce, or remarriage of a prospective planned giver or the addition of children or grandchildren to their families. Some other events are calendar events, such as the beginning of the year, tax filings, prior to vacations, bonus time, and the like. Plans made after natural disasters; accidents causing loss of life; changes in federal, state, and municipal tax and other laws; and reviews of estate plans often include final gifts to charitable institutions. Many people decide that the time for them to make planned gifts is at retirement or at the death of a spouse.

Such events are crucial to making major gift decisions, and they happen constantly. In all newsletters or other information provided to those who give to the institution, charitable institutions should regularly include their legally incorporated names and addresses. In addition, givers should be told that planned gifts are welcomed and can be made by naming the charitable institution as the first, second, or last beneficiary for part or all of the proceeds from their wills and other estate-planning documents.

When such information is presented to them frequently enough, prospective planned givers begin to notice it. Then when the life events occur that cause people to make or change their wills or other estate plans, donors will remember seeing the legally incorporated name in the institution's publications and can share it with the attorney who may be preparing wills or other documents for them.

## WHAT TYPES OF PEOPLE CHOOSE WHICH GIFTS?

Since most planned givers are thinking people who face the financial hazards of life head on, often they opt to make revocable deferred gifts. In fact, most institutions receive more than two-thirds of all matured deferred gifts from revocable deferred gift arrangements. Informed gift planners know the alternative to a revocable gift is not necessarily an irrevocable gift but no gift at all.

Studies reveal that many institutions receive most of their deferred gifts from regular, small givers who are women and who have been giving regular small amounts for some time. They are now in the old and old-old categories of life. In fact, the ideal deferred-giving prospects are unmarried women over age 70. Not only do they have a need to give, but many have received major assets upon the deaths of

54

their husbands, parents, or other relatives. The unlimited marital deduction for estate tax purposes, the fact that women, on average, live more than seven years longer than their husbands of the same age also accounts for this. At the widow's death these assets can be given to the institution(s) she chooses; often it is the one(s) she and her spouse had agreed to make a bequest to during their life together.

As mentioned, bequests from wills and trusts usually are made by people who are past age 70. This doesn't mean that wills or trusts made at earlier ages don't include bequests. However, when people get older, they tend to change or amend their wills or other estate transfer documents. The decision to give at death is often made in the later years when people review their plans for estate distribution.

## QUALIFIED PROSPECTIVE PLANNED GIVERS

People must have all of the following characteristics in order to be considered prospective planned givers:

1. Confidence in the leadership and belief in the mission of the institution.
2. Assets to fund the gift they choose to make.
3. Sets a date to meet with the charitable gift planner.
4. Motivation to give, and willingness to discuss the matter.

Unless people have confidence in the institution's board of trustees, the management, and the planned giving executive, they are not likely to be planned giving prospects. People who don't have discretionary assets are not prospective planned givers, at least for the present. People cannot discuss gift possibilities unless they are willing to see the charitable gift planner. And the lack of motivation eventually will cancel out all hopes of the person ever making a major current or deferred gift.

It is important to all concerned for the charitable gift planner to do enough research to determine the feasibility of contacting each individual. Donor research can provide many answers. An important part of the research is to try to determine if there is a person in the prospect's life who would be the primary and secondary influence when considering making a major current or deferred planned gift.

Major planned gifts result when prospective givers are satisfied that recipient institutions are rendering worthwhile services now and will continue to do so in the future. For example, the Church Health Center in Memphis has for nearly a decade provided quality health care for the working poor in the community. Volunteers (medical professionals and others) care for the patients, and an increasing number of volunteers have become active donors who support the center and make it work.

Recently a revolutionary program, which will have a far-reaching impact, was announced that would initially require $4,000,000 for capital purposes. Because of the confidence in the center's leadership, local foundations and a few individuals quickly committed funds needed. This successful start occurred because the chief executive officer had a dream that he successfully communicated to the trustees, and together they made it a mission. When the vision was well communicated, leaders in high places responded by contributing time, knowledge, and money. The Church Health Center's case for giving is in place, and other givers will follow in the months and years ahead to provide income to continue paying for operations and capital needs and for building an endowment.

How professional staff people communicate the vision and mission of their institutions helps givers decide when, what, and how to give. When employees charged with delivering services that help people solve their emotional, intellectual, physical, psychological, financial, spiritual, and other problems do their jobs well, their actions will determine, to a large extent, whether people will consider making major planned gifts.

## CONCLUSION

It is important for charitable gift planners to research the beginning of their institution and learn all they can about the founders' original vision. What was the big idea? What has happened since the beginning? What was the original mission and how has it been carried out? Chances are, major current and deferred planned givers will know this information. An executive recently told me about taking the planned giving job at a small college with over 100 years of history. She said when she visited an elderly donor, she was asked about the building named for a grandparent. She was embarrassed because she had not taken the time to learn the history of that building and why it was named as it was. Those who seek planned gifts must know the history of named gifts.

People become interested in making a planned gift when they believe their gift will impact a part of the institution's mission to others. They must, of course, trust the institution's leadership, have assets to give, and be willing to consider giving. But the institution and the gift planner always must be ready for the gift to happen and know how to acknowledge it, recognize the giver, and look for memorial opportunities.

# 5 ▼ Why People Make Planned Gifts

## GIVING IS A JOYFUL WAY OF LIFE

Gift planners have little or nothing to sell unless it is the pleasure people receive from giving. Giving is a voluntary act—not something people can be pushed into doing. Those who make current and deferred planned gifts receive a satisfaction that is not possible for nongivers to understand easily. Few experiences give one the joy motivated givers receive when making significant gifts that will be used to help other people. Charitable gift planners working with prospective planned givers really cannot understand what is going on in the giver's mind without personally experiencing the joy of giving.

The built-in need to give is seen in all strata of society. Affluent Americans have more money than they need or want. Some of them are channeling some of their wealth into service for others with tremendous benefits in personal satisfaction.

As important as it is for people to know that their gifts are made in the most effective ways possible and to be aware of how their gifts are used, the idea of making major current or deferred planned gifts begins in the emotions. But the gifts are not completed until the intellect "signs off" on how much to give, what to give (cash or other property), the timing, and the way gifts are to be transferred. It is more important for planners to determine *why* gifts are being made than the *what*, *when*, or *how* of the gift. Working out the tax implications often is the final act in completing planned gifts. Moreover, compared to the emotional concerns, the tax implications and other technical aspects of giving are relatively unimportant to most motivated planned givers.

To see the importance of the "why" of the gift, note the following example. A woman from a midwestern city said she had been the beneficiary of three different wills. She was the last member of her family still alive. Her health was such that she was unable to manage her property. When she gave most of this property in exchange for a lifetime income, she exclaimed enthusiastically, "Now the burden has been lifted."

A charitable institution benefits from planned gifts in many ways. For example, a donor who has a long-standing interest in an overseas mission agency gives because of his interest in that work but also realizes that part of the gift benefits the at-home support staff and the nationals in the foreign countries where the missionaries are serving. When gifts are made to children's homes, private schools, retirement communities, hospitals, and other institutions, charitable giving actually may reduce the government's role in caring for the people served.

## MOTIVATIONS FOR GIVING

With this background in mind, let us consider some of the motivations that cause people to give: Love, hate, fear, guilt, emulation, obligation, abundance, gratitude, recognition and memorials, and tax deductions.

Gifts are made because people *love or care* for others and

the interests of people who are served by the charitable institution. Wouldn't it be wonderful if the sole motivation for
giving was love for other people? For many, it *is* a major motivation in making gifts. Love, however, is by no means everyone's motivation.

Surprising as it sounds, there are cases where *hate* is the
motivation for giving. The word "hate" is a bit strong, but it
is nevertheless a motivation that has caused people to ex-
clude even close relatives from inheritances and to make
charitable transfers. I once heard a widower say to his two
children, "If you don't quit bothering me about the money
your mother left, I will give it all to charity." Many very old
people complain that their children and grandchildren do
not have time or do not care for them. Some people leave
their money to charity rather than to children who have disappointed them, done something wrong, been an embarrass-
ment, refused to work, married the wrong person, or didn't
marry at all.

Some give because of *fear* or superstition. A farmer could
believe that giving would influence the amount of rainfall, or
someone could think the health of loved ones depended on
giving.

We sometimes give because of *guilt*, our sins of commission and omission. People who have received the assets they
own from less-than-worthy activities and practices may be
giving to salve their consciences.

I grew up in the cotton fields of northeast Arkansas during the Great Depression. Landowners sometimes exacted
usurious interest charges from sharecroppers. Sharecroppers bought seed and fertilizer from landowners, ginned
their cotton at the landowners' gins, and sold the baled cotton and the seeds at the landowners' prices. (Tennessee Ernie
Ford explained the condition pretty well when he sang, "I
load sixteen tons and what do I get, another day older and
deeper in debt.") When landowners gave to support the

church (which some reportedly did), guilt could have been a motivating factor.

Guilt is still prevalent, but today it is dressed in different clothing. For example, people who own rodent-infested ghetto apartments and collect exorbitant rents from the poor may give some of their profits to worthy causes due to similar motivations.

People sometimes give to *emulate* others who give; also, they may give because they are urged to do so by someone they respect. One giver will give to a friend's cause and will obligate the friend to support a specified cause. "I gave $1,000 to your cause—now you owe me one, give to mine." Some people give because they are asked by people they respect—a friend or person of social or business prominence. Some large gifts come to institutions because the right person asks the right prospect for the right amount at the right time for the right purpose and offers the donor the right way to give.

A friend who is also a member of "our group" may press another to give out of *obligation*. Some institutions attempt to make members feel a responsibility to give through a challenge made to them to give whatever may be considered their "fair share." In some institutions this works well; in others, donors are turned off by talk of their "share." When giving becomes an obligation, people can lose the pleasure of giving.

"I have more than I need." Because some prospective givers have been blessed with *abundance*, they want to make gifts to carefully selected institution(s). Gift planners can be extremely helpful to those who want to give because of what they consider to be an "overflow" of assets.

Some people seem to have an unusual ability to know not only what investments to buy but when to sell at a profit. They accumulate far more than they ever expected and give because they have been so fortunate. Sometimes people give gifts of the excess in appreciation for their success.

*Gratitude* for having been served is one of the most marketable reasons for giving. People may give because they, or those close to them, have benefited from the institution's program. Just think of how educational, health care, religious, and all other worthy organizations have served individuals. Gift planners can open doors to a number of the people who have been served by their institutions.

Leaders of nonprofit institutions are unique in their ability to give *recognition* and establish *memorials*. One of the greatest hungers humans experience is for recognition. Many years ago while attending a convention I heard someone say, "Ninety-eight percent of the people in America go to bed hungry every night for recognition." Memorial gifts provide recognition not only for those who are being memorialized but also for those making the gifts.

*Tax deductions* are the least important of all the motivations for giving, but they can be very important to those who are already motivated to give. Tax deductions make it possible for motivated people to give more without increasing the cost of their giving, or they can give the same amounts and reduce the cost of their gifts. When people make gifts without considering the tax consequences, they exercise poor stewardship. However, giving solely for tax purposes may be a poor motive.

People who file the short federal income-tax return—approximately 70 percent of those filing—cannot itemize and deduct their gifts. Consequently, institutions need to be careful when promoting tax-deductible giving opportunities to rank-and-file constituents.

While tax-deductible giving is important to all institutions receiving charitable contributions, trustees and management need to develop programs of such quality that people will support their mission even if tax deductions are not available.

## WHY PEOPLE GIVE

Human beings are complex, beautiful, unique creatures. An individual's life experiences make up a collection of memories, perceptions, patterns, and emotions. There is no set formula for determining why people do the things they do. As a general rule, although people often think that they have carefully thought through their decisions to give, in fact often we give impulsively and some of us are habitual givers. Emotion is the river on which logic flows.

Planned givers are special people who want to make charitable gifts in the most effective ways possible. They obtain professional help in order to understand how to give more effectively. Planned givers also want to understand how recipient charitable institutions will use their gifts.

When charitable gift planners do adequate research before visiting prospective planned givers, they probably will gain some understanding as to why the prospect(s) may be considering giving at that particular time. Understanding givers' motivations will go a long way toward helping them decide the amount, the form, and the timing of their gifts.

# 6 ▼ What Planned Givers Want to Keep When They Give

What people want to give when they make a planned gift is one question, but what they want to keep is another of equal importance. Both must be considered in gift-planning transactions. What donors are willing to give usually is not nearly as important to them as what they want to keep. Their primary concerns are maintaining their financial security while retaining their economic freedom. As people get older, these concerns become more important. Therefore, charitable gift planners must learn early in each gift-planning interview what financial security and economic freedom mean to prospective planned givers.

Financial security usually means having enough assets to provide for future needs; economic freedom means that people are free to give or keep or do whatever they please with what they own.

## FOUR FINANCIAL HAZARDS

Before engineers charged with designing a bridge finally decide what kind of bridge to build, first they must determine what will destroy the bridge. Is high wind velocity a threat in the area? Will increased traffic, heavy equipment, and large traffic destroy the bridge? Just as engineers know the hazards that will destroy their bridge, charitable gift planners and others involved in the charitable estate- and gift-planning process must understand and consider what hazards can destroy people financially.

All people face the same four financial hazards in life: (1) having emergencies without enough savings or insurance to carry them through this time; (2) dying too soon before accumulating enough assets to take care of their survivors; (3) becoming totally and permanently disabled and not having enough assets to care for themselves and their family; and (4) living too long and not having enough savings to continue an adequate income through the retirement years.

Prospective planned givers probably will not make major current and deferred gifts unless they are satisfied that they can maintain their financial security and retain their economic freedom should they face any of these four hazards. Let's look at each hazard in the order people are most likely to face them during life.

## Unexpected Emergencies

Unexpected financial emergencies constitute the first hazard. Almost anything can happen at any time, from the beginning until the end of life. Some common emergencies we face are legal judgments arising from personal or other liabilities not covered by insurance; accidents and illnesses; inflation affecting retirees on fixed incomes; theft of assets; investment losses; failure of financial service companies; unexpected long-term care of aged parents; war; and storms, floods, and other acts of God. Most people can expect to have some of these emergencies, and it is important for planners to anticipate that prospective planned givers may experience them.

These emergencies can be covered, at least to some extent, by regular savings, catastrophic health insurance, personal and auto liability insurance, and fire and other insurance.

## Dying Without Leaving Enough Assets to Care for Survivors

The second and probably the most critical of the four financial hazards, especially to younger families, is the concern about providing adequate income to surviving spouses, children, and any other dependents. One way to address this problem is through the purchase of substantial amounts of life insurance (renewable term or decreasing term policies will satisfy this need in the early years for most couples), which can be arranged to continue income to surviving family members at death.

## Permanent Disability

The third financial hazard raises the question of what happens when the family wage-earner(s) or spouse becomes totally and permanently disabled. Permanent disability often causes a family to carry a heavier financial load than it would if the person had died. Other family members must provide income for themselves while paying the cost of care for the permanently disabled wage-earner. Disability and other insurance along with social security can help with the financial needs of the disabled.

## Having Inadequate Savings to Continue Income Through Retirement Years

The fourth financial hazard is reaching retirement age without having enough accumulated savings to care for the retiree and family member(s) for life. Many people save for retirement, but savings may be inadequate because of accident or illness, inflation, market losses, theft, and other events.

It is difficult to determine which financial hazard is the most important. At different stages of life, different hazards are more important. Charitable gift planners must be aware of the specific hazards and how they affect individuals and families at different stages of life.

Charitable gift planners must be of the highest integrity. Professional gift planners must not accept funds irrevocably from prospective planned givers if making the gift will adversely affect givers' financial security and economic freedom. Gifts still can be made, but advisors must carefully consider the method needed to help ensure or even enhance givers' security. Most likely, gifts can be completed using revocable gift arrangements such as wills, revocable living trusts, life insurance and annuity policies, retirement plan assets, or other contractual transfer arrangements. Gift planners should have a basic knowledge of financial products that could provide planned givers with an extra measure of stability before they risk taking away givers' security through giving in the wrong way. Note: Advisors do not have to master all the different kinds of property; rather they should learn enough to talk about the subject and know when to refer potential givers to professionals for advice.

Here are some basic steps most people can take that will help protect them against the financial hazards of life:

## 1. Emergencies

To survive emergencies, individuals probably will want to be protected by catastrophic major medical insurance to pay for costly accidents and illnesses, have adequate automobile and personal liability insurance, and have a reserve equal to 6 to 12 months' salary.

An old friend told me many years ago that if every family would accumulate six months' salary, they could dispense of double-digit interest rates charged and put the loan sharks out of business. I discovered early in life that stockpiling such a nest egg was possible, therefore, I was able to purchase household appliances and other high-price items a family needs with cash. Rather than paying a lender, I replenished my account by making the payments to that fund. It also made it possible for me to purchase insurance of all kinds at reduced premiums because I was able to accept higher deductibles by carrying that risk myself.

### 2. Disability

To help people survive total and permanent disability, individuals can purchase disability income insurance to replace some of the monthly income lost while disabled. When people become totally and permanently disabled, social security payments add to their security after a waiting period. Veterans who have an ascertainable service-connected disability may be eligible to receive Veteran's Administration benefits. Whatever assets have been accumulated by the time disability commences will help fund the family budget through the waiting periods required before insurance and other benefits commence.

### 3. Retirement

To ensure a retirement free from financial hardship, individuals must start planning and saving early in life. Most 25-year-olds will live to retire at the age of 65, but only a few will have accumulated enough assets without outside help to continue their standard of living. In addition, successful investments will add to retirement income. At birth we face certain life stages that impact us financially. From birth until we are 18 to 25, we are at least partially dependent on others for financial support. These are the learning years. From the time we start working until retirement, we are in the earning years. During this time we have to deliberately reduce our standard of living in order to save for a reasonable standard of living later. When we reach retirement years without having saved enough of our income to assure our future, these can be the yearning years.

## 4. Death

The least expensive and probably most certain way for most people to guarantee security for a family at the death of the family wage-earner(s), especially in the early years, is through the purchase of life insurance. As assets are accumulated, they can replace life insurance.

## GIFT PLANNERS' RESPONSES TO THESE FEARS

Prospective planned givers who are near or in their retirement years are very sensitive to the four financial hazards and do what they can to protect themselves against potential losses that could affect them during retirement. As a result, they usually make planned gift decisions carefully. Most older people are reluctant to fund planned gifts that will, in any way, leave them unable to get their assets, if and when they are needed. Gift planners who present ideas using the tax-oriented plans may be tempted to offer only irrevocable giving plans, such as charitable gift annuities, pooled income plans, life estate contracts, and charitable remainder annuity trusts or unitrusts; however, it may be safer for the individual to make only a revocable gift arrangement. Many planned gifts have been lost because of gift planners' failure to fully understand the needs of prospective planned givers and their surviving family members for financial security and economic freedom. Gift planners need to have little concern when the planned gift arrangement is revocable because the

## Exhibit 6.1   A Test for Givers

It is important for charitable gift planners to always urge prospective planned givers to take a test that quizzes them on four aspects of their intended gift: Will you need any of these assets:

1. If you become totally and permanently disabled?
2. In the event of the death of a family member?
3. During retirement?
4. If you have a financial emergency?

majority of deferred gift maturities are delivered to charities through revocable giving plans.

## QUESTIONS TO ASK PROSPECTIVE PLANNED GIVERS

Charitable gift planners and givers' advisors should urge their donor/clients to consider carefully their answers to the next four questions before completing an irrevocable gift arrangement:

1. In the event of an emergency, will you need the assets being placed in this irrevocable agreement?
2. If you become totally and permanently disabled, will you need the assets being placed in this irrevocable agreement?
3. When you retire, will you have adequate resources to sustain you without using the funds placed in this irrevocable gift arrangement?
4. At your death, will you be able to provide security for your family without using the funds placed in this irrevocable gift arrangement?

Any yes answer is enough to play it safe and help people make *revocable* gift arrangements.

When dealing with older people, often it is helpful for gift planners to assume that they are dealing with aged parents or grandparents and treat the prospective planned givers accordingly.

Charitable gift planners should not give specific advice on legal matters, or on insurance or other financial products. Planners always should urge prospective planned givers to consult with their own advisors for specific opinions.

In the final analysis, the financial security and economic freedom of prospective givers must be protected; charitable gift planners can do so by recognizing the existence of people's needs for financial security and economic freedom.

# III ▼ THE GIFT PLANNER

In this section we look at who helps the planned givers make their gifts.

Chapter 7 discusses five types of individual gift planners and those corporate entities most interested in providing services to help people complete major current and deferred planned gifts. Who are they, what do they do, and how do they serve prospective givers and institutions? How is each compensated, and how can they work together to help prospective planned givers make major current and deferred gifts to the institution(s) of their choice?

Other chapters deal with what givers and management should expect from a gift planner, how gift planning has evolved, and the hopes that gift planners have for the future.

# The Planners Who Help People Make Planned Gifts

Many people who employ advisors to help them plan their estates have a desire to make major gifts at death. They want to give something back to society and wish to know the best ways to arrange their gifts. It's important for charitable gift planners to work hand in hand with allied professionals to coordinate the gift-giving and estate-planning process. First, however, charitable gift planners must seek planned givers' permission prior to contacting any of their advisors. Many different advisors make up the gift-planning team.

This chapter is about the institutions and individuals involved in assisting donors/clients complete major current and/or deferred planned gifts. The functions and financial interests of each of the individuals and institutions that provide charitable estate- and gift-planning services to their donor/clients who are considering gifts to America's charitable institutions are discussed. It is worth noting that if it were not for the plans of giving created by the Tax Reform Act of 1969, which include charitable remainder trusts and other irrevocable gift arrangements, and the existence of federal income-, gift-, and estate-tax benefits to donors, few charitable gift planners, planned giving consultants, financial

service institutions, community foundations, trust companies, financial planners, attorneys, or accountants would
have much interest in the charitable estate- and gift-planning
process as we know it today. Who these individuals and financial institutions are, the services they render to prospective planned givers, and how they are compensated for their
services is the thrust of this chapter.

## CHARITABLE GIFT PLANNERS (EMPLOYEES OF CHARITABLE INSTITUTIONS)

When charitable institutions began, trustees and management people who had other responsibilities also were responsible for fund raising. They were charged with
acquiring all kinds of gifts—regular small gifts, special gifts,
and occasionally major current and deferred gifts—to fund
their charitable institutions. They were generalists and did
not give much time or thought to the solicitation of deferred
gifts.

I was first employed by an international Christian organization in 1959. The position was created for the purpose of
encouraging bequests through wills. I spent all of my time
developing a program to encourage gifts from across the
United States and Canada that matured at the death of
donors. At that time only a few charitable institutions employed people to work full time encouraging gifts through
wills and other deferred giving plans.

Without much effort on anyone's part during the 1960s
and l970s, institutions received some deferred gifts, most of
them through wills. Incidentally, even after all our efforts to
educate the American public about plans of giving that offer
federal income-tax benefits, as of early 1998, wills still provide most of the total deferred gift maturities received by
America's charitable institutions. I predict gifts maturing

through wills should continue to be the primary source of deferred gift income right into the twenty-first century.

Other deferred giving plans discussed with people in the 1960s and 1970s were revocable living trusts, life income plans, tax-exempt life income plans, life estate contracts, gift annuities, and short-term charitable trusts (two-year Clifford-type trusts). In addition, people were urged to name the institutions as beneficiaries in retirement plans, life insurance policies, and savings and loan association and bank products.

At that time some managers realized that perhaps they could do more to encourage more deferred giving. Realizing the importance of deferred gifts to the future of their institutions, management began to employ special people to seek out such gifts. After the Tax Reform Act of 1969, which created new plans of giving, many trustees and management became even more convinced that their future financial security depended more and more on having an active deferred giving program. Specialists in deferred giving began to use the words "planned giving" as part of their job titles. However, and unfortunately, some of them began "selling" planned gifts as commodities, even as "good" investments. Many potential planned gifts have been lost because the vehicle of giving was emphasized instead of the human relations aspect of making gifts. Some institutions and their planned giving staff continue selling gift annuities, pooled income plans, and charitable remainder trusts as commodities and investments rather than presenting them as ways to give to motivated people.

The use of the term "planned giving" increased following the enactment of the Tax Reform Act of 1969. After this act, the leadership in some organizations employed development people who would be able to help interested givers complete both current and deferred planned gifts.

Now, after nearly three decades, bequests continue to be more productive in most institutions than all other deferred

giving plans combined, especially in institutions with successful long-term planned giving programs. When wills
awareness programs are the centerpiece, rather than a pe-
ripheral focus, of charitable institutions' planned giving programs, planned giving maturities from wills should equal
about twice the total amount received from all other deferred
giving plans.

To make this happen, today's charitable gift planners—
those employed and compensated by nonprofit institutions—
need to be able to coordinate the charitable estate- and
gift-planning process. Charitable gift planners must change
from being purveyors of deferred planned giving "vehicles"
to working comfortably with prospective planned givers who
are motivated to make current or deferred planned gifts or
both. The future is bright for charitable gift planners who are
able to coordinate the charitable estate and gift planning
process and work with any of the professional advisors of
those interested in giving.

Charitable gift planners are not the only ones who help
people complete planned gifts. At times many allied professionals also may be "gift planners." The following sections
describe various other professionals and how they serve their
clients (who may also be donors).

## INDEPENDENT PLANNED GIVING CONSULTANTS

The managements of some charities engage the services of
consultants to assist some of their planned giving prospects in
developing their estate plans. Charitable institutions offer the
services of these consultants to selected donors who likely will
make major planned gifts by naming the institutions as the remainderman in trusts and/or as a beneficiary in wills and
other estate-planning arrangements. These consultants are

compensated by the charitable institutions. However, management must be vigilant to ensure that those consultants that are licensed to sell life insurance and/or securities or offer financial management services, do not offer them to these donors.

There are some problems associated with the contact-by-consultant approach. First, could the fees paid to consultants delivering estate-planning services by a tax-exempt charitable institution be considered reportable income by givers who were assisted?

For example, suppose a 75-year-old wealthy donor indicated she may be willing to consider making an estate gift to a charitable institution. The institution doesn't have a competent staff person who is capable of assisting her. The leadership of the institution believes it has a good prospect for what could be a substantial deferred gift. The institution asks an independent consultant to go to the donor's home, unaccompanied by an official of the institution or by an unpaid volunteer, to interview her, make recommendations, and help her design an estate plan that, it is hoped, might include a major deferred gift. The interview(s) were successful and she established a charitable remainder annuity trust for $500,000. The charitable institution pays the consultant $15,000 for assisting the donor with her estate plan. Two questions arise: (1) Is the fee reportable income by the donor and does the charity have to report this fee as income paid to her? and (2) Has the charity compromised its relationship with this donor by failing to have a trustee or employee accompany the consultant on the visit(s)?

Even though charitable institutions are named as the beneficiaries in charitable remainder trusts, by using independent planned giving consultants the institutions may lose the opportunity for future contact with prospective planned givers. Consultants establish relationships with donors that have the implied blessing and endorsement of the nonprofit institution's trustees and the chief executive officer; it may be difficult for future gift planning personnel to establish their own relationships with these important givers.

In the long run, charitable institutions are best served when their own staff builds indigenous charitable gift-planning programs. The staff represents and understands the vision, mission, and case for giving to the charity. Ideally, the gift-planning personnel are managers who can help lead institutions as they plan, communicate, manage, and evaluate their own planned giving program—a program that serves the needs of prospective planned givers while building vital relationships with their most important donors. Instead of having outsiders contacting its best givers, the institution's insiders will work with them and their own counsel by coordinating the charitable estate- and gift-planning process rather than attempting to do estate-planning themselves.

When I first became a charitable gift consultant, I worked for several institutions at once. My goal was to help management organize, develop their planned giving marketing programs, respond to inquiries, and visit with prospective planned givers to help them complete planned gifts. After a few years I realized that while I had helped people make gifts to the institutions, management didn't have a relationship with some of their best prospective planned givers. I discovered the indigenous principle and stopped visiting with prospective donors unless I was accompanied by a staff member from the client institution. Thereafter my career changed. My consulting was limited to helping the leadership of client organizations build indigenous planned giving programs that fit the "personality" of their institutions and staffed by full-time employees of the institutions who could establish ongoing relationships while securing current and deferred planned gifts.

Farsighted trustees and management will make their planned giving programs an integral part of their institution's mission. They will budget enough money annually and will be patient long enough (for three to seven years) for the deferred giving part of their planned giving program to begin to produce net income.

## FINANCIAL PLANNERS

While charitable gift planning was evolving, financial planning was also changing. In the 1950s, the financial planning I did, as a life insurance agent, often centered around the sale of life insurance policies. In a few years, many agents began to venture into selling mutual funds and other financial products. It became apparent to many of us that the future and the success of life insurance agents would depend on their becoming more proficient in marketing a variety of products.

Awareness of these changes caused many financial planners to start learning more about the importance of life insurance in overall estate planning. This heightened interest in estate analysis led to a better understanding of property and forms of business ownership. As planners learned more about securities and mutual funds as well as real estate and retirement plans, they realized they also needed to know more about trusts, foundations, and charitable institutions. Today, the majority of financial planners are employees or commissioned sales agents for financial service companies, including those companies that sell life insurance and securities. Some attorneys and certified public accountants also represent themselves to the public as financial planners.

Some financial planners believe planned giving is limited to what people over age 55 do to create charitable remainder trusts. These trusts are generally funded with highly appreciated assets by those who want to: avoid the payment of capital-gains taxes, receive a whopping charitable deduction on their federal income-tax return, receive a joint and survivor-ship lifetime income (if a couple), have favorable tax treatment on the annual income received, and/or leave the charitable remainder interest to the charity at death. Through the purchase of a last-to-die life insurance policy on the life or lives of the donor(s), the family could receive policy proceeds equal to the amount initially placed in the trust. Such an arrangement appeals to many financial planners and their clients.

In reality, clients who are over age 70 and in the highest federal income- and estate-tax brackets who want to give to charitable institutions but also want income for life are the best prospects for establishing charitable remainder trusts. Establishing these trusts for a term of years is also appealing for younger people; they designate the income to another beneficiary with the charitable remainder becoming a gift to a charity at the end of the trust term.

Because of favorable tax benefits, the cost of making charitable gifts can be reduced. Financial planners who work closely with their clients know their financial situations well, and by mentioning tax benefits at the right time, eventually they are able to help their clients make major charitable gifts. Employees of charitable institutions already may have motivated these clients to give. Upon learning of a client's interests in giving, financial planners may be in a better position than anyone else to help clients finally take action and bring into being a substantial present or future gift to the charitable institutions of their choice.

Tax laws were not designed to help people make money by giving it away. Giving always must cost donors something, or it is not a gift. What givers actually receive in exchange are the emotional or spiritual benefits from making gifts that will benefit others in society. When planners emphasize only the tax advantages, givers lose the pure joy of giving. Financial planners serve their clients well indeed when they help them make their gift of a lifetime to the institution(s) of their choice. Financial planners receive satisfaction when givers are helped to realize their own need to give.

Financial planners and charitable gift planners can work together very effectively when the formers' clients are also interested in the latters' institution. Both planners must put forth every effort to work together effectively. Neither planner should expect the other to provide names of clients/donors or to use the services of each other to make presentations designed to sell products to prospective donors, or to sell gift plans to financial clients. Charitable institutions are well advised to avoid any fund-raising efforts offered to them by any individual and/or institution if participating prospective planned givers are likely to assume an implied endorsement. After all, it is doubtful that financial service companies and financial planners would provide such endorsements to charitable gift planners.

Financial planners can benefit financially in several ways when their clients create charitable remainder trusts and charitable lead trusts. Licensed financial planners are able to receive commissions and renewal fees from the sale of wealth replacement and other family or business life insurance policies that may result from the relationship. They also may receive commissions or finders' fees when they sell securities or other property to those who manage the investment and reinvestment of trust assets.

Sometimes financial planners can steer their clients' gifts to charities they favor. Some have asked institutional management to pay for the preparation of trust documents, environmental appraisals, and other expenses connected with gift transactions. A few even have asked the charity to pay them finders' fees.

Financial planners can add much to the future of charitable institutions and serve their clients well by informing them of ways to give to those institutions. The most popular ways they can suggest to their clients to name charities include beneficiary designations for (1) part or all of the proceeds in life insurance policies (new and existing); (2) IRAs and other retirement plans; and (3) wills, contracts, and trust arrangements. They also can suggest adding the names of institutions following the depositor's name on certificates of deposit offered by banks, credit unions, and savings and loan associations.

## FINANCIAL SERVICE CORPORATIONS

In recent years charitable gift planning has become a very important subject to financial service companies. Some of these institutions have incorporated tax-exempt charitable entities in order to receive from their customers funds that will be used to establish charitable remainder trusts and other federal tax-oriented planned giving arrangements.

These charitable gift funds appear to me to be tax-exempt "subsidiaries" of for-profit corporations. The institution's sales staff is able to sell securities, including mutual funds that will be used to fund charitable remainder trusts, charitable lead trusts, pooled income funds, donor-advised funds, and other planned giving arrangements for the lives of their customers/donors. Through these tax-exempt funds, donors are able to name qualified charitable institutions as charitable remainder beneficiaries, and the financial service company assumes the management of trust assets for the life or lives of the trustors and survivors.

Financial service companies benefit by having their employees and other security salespeople offer to their clients and customers, for a fee, the services of their nonprofit "subsidiaries" that will receive, invest, reinvest, and distribute funds to qualified charities. The companies are compensated by profits realized from fees built into their mutual fund products and by ongoing management fees. Should the charity named as the beneficiary in the trust not be in existence at the death of trustors, the assets would be distributed to another qualified charity chosen by the trustees of the nonprofit "subsidiary" of the for-profit financial service company.

Some people question whether for-profit organizations should be able to create tax-exempt entities that are used to funnel business to "parent" for-profit financial service institutions. They believe this type of institution should not be legally exempt from taxation because of lack of charitable purpose and a misuse of the nonprofit status. While only a few major financial service corporations have established these charitable funds, many other mutual fund companies, banks, and other financial service companies may feel compelled to do so as a defensive business move, to round out their offering of services to their customers. By allowing for-profit companies to use subsidiary nonprofit organizations as feeders to their businesses, government officials who approved did not act in the best interest of society. While these nonprofit or tax-exempt subsidiaries continue to deliver many millions of dollars to charitable institutions, it is a misuse of tax law when nonprofit entities are used to sell services of for-profit corporations. I hope legislative bodies will take another look at what is happening in this arena.

## TRUST COMPANIES

Trust departments provide a wide variety of services for prospective planned givers. These corporate entities have been involved in major gift planning long before planned giving became a part of charitable institutions' financial development programs, and offer several other desirable features, including continuity, objectivity, and specificity.

Regarding continuity, corporate trustees, custodians, agents, and executors never die, get sick, move out of town, or cause the trustor to worry about other problems that may be associated with naming individuals to these positions.

Because they are not related to the planned giver, trust companies and bank trust departments tend to be more objective than individuals. They will follow the directives of the trust document and are not subject to any of the informal pressures that individuals sometimes encounter.

In addition, corporate trustees have professional investment managers who will tailor portfolios to the specific needs of the individual.

Trust companies and bank trust departments can serve as trustees of charitable remainder trusts, revocable and irrevocable living trusts, trusts under wills, executors of estates, investment advisors, custodians, and escrow agents. They also can advise planned givers on tax matters, estate planning, and financial planning.

Corporate trustees are compensated based on a percentage of the market value of the account as well as the amount of responsibility they assume.

It is imperative for charitable gift planners, financial planners, and others to urge prospective planned givers to seek advice from their own legal and/or other counsel before finalizing major planned gifts. In fact, all charitable gift planners must provide a statement in writing advising planned givers to check any proposals for making planned gifts with their own advisors.

## COMMUNITY FOUNDATIONS

Community foundations are established to help generous people give to nonprofit institutions. The foundations receive major current and deferred gifts from local citizens who have charitable giving interests. The advised account idea helps those who might otherwise establish private foundations enjoy the benefits of a foundation without having the responsibility for its management. The advised account is a fund given to a community foundation and perhaps to other foundations created by major church bodies. The donor reserves the right to advise the foundation to make grants to selected beneficiaries. The financial service company gift fund works much the same—the original donor is only an advisor and is unable to demand that gifts be directed to charities they name. Community foundations make their greatest impact by receiving funds given for the designated funding of operating charitable organizations. These foundations are funded with gifts from interested people and are run by annual administrative charges.

## CERTIFIED PUBLIC ACCOUNTANTS

Over the years, certified public accountants (CPAs) often have been able to advise donors when they begin thinking about making major current or deferred planned gifts. Having provided tax counsel and prepared federal, state, and other income, gift, and estate tax returns for their clients, they usually know the kind and value of their clients' accumulated assets, their income, and their patterns of giving. More than likely they also understand the motivations behind their clients' benevolence.

Accountants often are involved in the early stages of the giving process. A few years ago I invited a friend to lunch to discuss giving to an institution in which both of us were interested. I said to him, "What would you think about making a substantial gift to the project under consideration?" He responded by asking "How much is substantial?" I told him $30,000. "I'll do it if my CPA thinks I can afford it." In a few days he told me that his CPA told him that it would be much better if the gift were $300 a month for ten years. I recall another person calling to tell me that her accountant had told her she could give $17,000 before the end of the year and she would be sending some securities. CPAs are compensated by agreed-upon fees.

## ATTORNEYS

Attorneys have been heavily involved in planned giving from the time the first wills benefiting charities were made up to the present. Charitable institutions are indebted to attorneys for the help they have given clients who want to give. In fact, before most institutions ever thought of planned giving programs, attorneys were facilitating gifts. Many gift planners have developed amicable relationships with attorneys and work with legal counsel to help them accomplish their own goals. Attorneys are compensated by agreed-upon fees. I always suggest to prospective planned givers that they seek the help of their own legal counsel to assist them in accomplishing their goals. (For the attorney's view of the charitable estate and gift planning process, see Exhibit 7.1.)

## ALLIED PROFESSIONALS AND CHARITABLE GIFT PLANNERS WORKING TOGETHER IN THE GIFT PLANNING PROCESS

In many institutions, irrevocable charitable remainder trusts and other federal income tax-oriented giving plans combined deliver only about one-third of the total deferred gift dollars each year. The total value of maturities received from irrevocable agreements, such as charitable remainder trusts since 1969, has been relatively unimportant to many charitable

## Exhibit 7.1   The Attorney's Role in Charitable Estate and Gift Planning

Attorneys are trained to represent their clients in a manner that is to the client's best interest. In order to properly represent clients in an estate planning or charitable gift-planning manner, attorneys must have knowledge of relevant state laws governing trusts and estates; common law and statutory rules relating to perpetuities and alienation of interests; and the fiduciary rights, powers, and responsibilities of executives and trustees.

Experience in planning estates, and the effective use of charitable components as a part thereof, should be prerequisite. Some charitable estate and gift planning involves alternate strategies to achieve income, gift, estate, and generation-skipping transfer benefits, familiarity with public and private foundation rules, family limited partnerships, testementary and inter vivos transfer rules, and the tax implications of grantor, beneficiary, and trustee rights and powers are essential.

To plan estates properly, attorneys must prepare all legal documents, including wills, trusts, deeds of gift, assignment et al., and they should coordinate and complete a successful plan by supervising the execution and filing of notices, receipts, documents, and tax returns, and making certain that every step has been completed and documented.

Most practitioners quote and bill for services based on hourly rates. However, it is not unusual for clients to request and receive quotations of a fixed price for a package of services, including the planning, documentation, coordination of advisors, and implementation of the plan. This is particularly true of cases in which the fees on an hourly basis might be expected to reach a high dollar amount.

Thomas R. Dyer
Attorney, Wyatt, Tarrant, and Combs
Memphis, Tennessee

## Exhibit 7.2  Total Bequests and Life Income Gifts to Selected Universities for 1996

|  | Bequests | Life Income Gifts | Totals | Percent Bequests |
|---|---|---|---|---|
| Brown University | $5,749,282 | $1,268,702 | $7,017,984 | 82% |
| University of California, Berkeley | 12,520,398 | 8,170,226 | 20,690,624 | 61% |
| University of Chicago | 13,810,784 | 3,460,379 | 17,271,163 | 80% |
| Columbia University | 13,144,125 | 8,537,341 | 21,681,466 | 61% |
| Cornell University | 21,435,973 | 13,735,090 | 35,171,063 | 61% |
| Dartmouth | 13,539,534 | 11,147,396 | 24,686,930 | 55% |
| University of Iowa | 27,071,587 | 6,525,347 | 33,596,934 | 81% |
| University of Michigan | 18,033,960 | 5,918,433 | 23,952,393 | 75% |
| Princeton University | 17,235,933 | 7,116,807 | 24,352,740 | 71% |
| Stanford University | 53,160,098 | 47,534,720 | 100,694,818 | 53% |
| Washington University | 21,564,422 | 3,596,223 | 25,160,645 | 86% |
| Yale University | 36,058,973 | 19,713,763 | 5,772,736 | 65% |
| Totals | $253,325,069 | $136,714,427 | $390,049,496 | 65% |

*Source:* Council for Aid to Education, "Voluntary Support of Education 1996" report.

institutions. The majority of deferred gift maturities have come to charities through the non–income-tax-oriented giving plans. It is unlikely that charitable remainder trusts will ever deliver large numbers of major deferred planned gifts because of the two needs people have: to give and to maintain their financial security and economic freedom.

That is why charitable gift planners who are employees of charitable institutions need to be able to coordinate the planning process. While not disinterested, they do not make a sale, receive a commission, or have another ax to grind. They can stay in touch with major givers and walk with them through life.

To illustrate the importance of bequests to educational institutions, the Council for Aid to Education in its report "Voluntary Support of Education 1996" noted that 39.3 percent of voluntary support was received from bequests and life income gifts. Bequests accounted for more than $1.5 billion, or 24.2 percent, while life income gifts provided over $953 million, or 15.1 percent. The figures in Exhibit 7.2 are taken from the council's report.

An average of 24.2 percent of total gifts to education came from bequests, while an average of only 15.1 percent came from other deferred gifts. These figures demonstrate how important it is for management to carefully review the results of the above-listed institutions in order to determine where to place their budgetary priorities when building a planned giving program in their institutions. Obviously, the desire of prospective givers to give revocably is much more important to the givers and to the institution when results are tallied.

# 8 ▼ Charitable Gift Planners: Who They Are

How do charitable gift planners see themselves? We are both individuals and members of a group, and our self-perception goes a long way toward defining our role. Here we explore what is required to be a charitable gift planner and what is required for charitable gift planning to become a profession.

Charitable gift planners do not have to be experienced professional fund raisers in order to succeed. Charitable gift planners are not, in the truest sense, fund raisers at all; the real fund raisers are those who carry out the mission of the institution; charitable gift planners gather the funds the fund raisers "produce."

## WHEN MANAGEMENT HIRES CHARITABLE GIFT PLANNERS

Before interviewing candidates for the position of charitable gift planner, the leadership needs to examine itself carefully, making certain the trustees, the chief executive officer, and all senior executives understand that they are the owners of the planned giving program. The management must make it clear that the program belongs to the leadership and the position being offered is as manager of the institution's program. The planned giving executive should not carry the burden of owning the planned giving program alone, rather he or she manages the leadership's planned giving program. When an institution's leadership really owns the planned giving program, they take a greater interest in making it successful. The success or failure of the program depends on both the leadership and the planned giving executive.

Leaders seeking to employ a charitable gift planner should:

- Look within the present staff for someone who is native to the institution and make certain he or she is committed to its mission. Charitable gift planners may have difficulty securing gift funds unless they are motivated by commitment to the institution and possess a strong human relations background.
- Look for a candidate who cares about older people, because they are the primary prospects who will make major current and deferred planned gifts to the institution.
- Look for a person with only a speaking acquaintance with tax law who understands it will be helpful, but expertise in the law is not required or necessary for candidates to become successful as charitable gift planners. A liberal arts education is helpful. In some instances, those who are technically oriented may not have the time to do a good job and keep abreast of tax law changes. While a speaking acquaintance with tax laws is important, knowing enough about tax law to render an opinion is unnecessary in most jobs.
- Look for someone who will spend more than half of the time out of the office in the presence of prospective planned givers. This should be made an important issue in the interview. Sometimes committee meetings, a comfortable office, and the overuse of the Internet robs planned giving executives of success.

- Look for a stable person who probably will continue in the job for at least five years.

Charitable gift planners must be students of human relations and learn to work with legal and other advisors of the prospective givers. This can be accomplished in part through training. Charitable gift planners can acquire a speaking acquaintance with legal, financial, and related fields of work, but this is not necessary for charitable gift planners to be able to "dot all the i's and cross all the t's" of tax laws, finance, accounting, wills, trusts, and other contracts.

Charitable gift planners are crying out to be recognized as members of a profession. In the last decade, approximately 100 planned giving councils have sprung up all around the United States and Canada. Through these councils, gift planners can share experiences and receive continuing education. But those of us working in planned giving still are not widely recognized as professionals by the general public.

According to *Webster's New Third International Dictionary*, a profession is: "A calling requiring recognized knowledge and often long and intensive preparation including instruction in skills and methods as well as in the scientific, historical, scholarly principles underlying such skills and methods, maintaining by force of organization or concerted opinion high standards of achievements and conduct, and committing its members to continued study and to a kind of work that has for its prime purpose the rendering of a public service."

Can charitable gift planners simultaneously serve prospective planned givers and the charitable institutions they represent? Planners have been trying to do so, but it is like walking on eggshells. Charitable gift planners must constantly balance the interests of both parties. They are paid employees attempting to serve prospective planned givers and charitable institutions at the same time. Hard questions surface that are difficult to answer, but they must be addressed early in the relationship between the leadership of the institution and the charitable gift planner.

Planners may wonder what is expected of them when responding to donors who want to consider making major current or deferred planned gifts to the charitable institution they represent. What do prospective planned givers expect from the planners who respond to their inquiries about planned gifts?

To answer these questions, charitable gift planners must clearly understand the basic fund-gathering philosophy of the trustees and management. For example, they need to know how much the management is willing to press people to give.

## OPPOSITE PRIORITIES

What are the nonprofit organization's priorities when seeking major current and deferred planned gifts? Generally, their needs, desires, or priorities are as follows: (1) to secure major current planned gifts of cash or other assets without any strings attached; (2) to be named the charitable remainderman in irrevocable charitable trusts or other gift arrangements; and (3) to be named as a beneficiary in wills or other revocable giving plans.

What are the priorities of most prospective planned givers when they consider making major current or deferred planned gifts? Generally, their needs, desires, or priorities are as follows: (1) to name the institution as a beneficiary in a will or other revocable giving plan; (2) to name the charitable institution as the charitable remainderman in irrevocable trusts or other giving plans; and (3) to make a major current planned gift of cash or other assets without any strings attached. Notice how the priorities of the charitable institution's leadership and prospective planned givers are opposite! (See Exhibit 8.1.)

As discussed elsewhere, prospective givers will first consider making their planned gifts revocable because they want to retain the option of having their money returned if they need or want it. In fact, they are willing to forgo tax deductions in order to make their commitments revocable, so they can keep their financial security and economic freedom. When prospective planned givers believe their financial well-being is not being compromised, they will consider making irrevocable life income arrangements, but generally this is a

### Exhibit 8.1   Priorities of Charitable Institution versus Priorities of Prospective Planned Giver

| Charitable Institution | | Prospective Planned Giver |
|---|---|---|
| 1. To secure major planned gifts without any strings attached. | vs. | 1. To name the institution as a beneficiary in a will or other revocable giving plan. |
| 2. To become named as a charitable remainderman (one who receives what is left in a trust) in an irrevocable charitable trust. | vs. | 2. To name the charitable institution as the charitable remainderman in irrevocable trusts or other giving plans. |
| 3. To be named a beneficiary in a will or other revocable giving plan. | vs. | 3. To make a major current planned gift of cash or other assets without any strings attached. |

second choice. Unless prospective planned givers have a great amount of intent to give, they will not sacrifice much financial security. They will want to be certain that they and their survivors or others will still have assets sufficient to continue living in the style to which they have been accustomed.

Charitable gift planners sometime find themselves in conflict because they know that the priorities of management and of those who give are in opposition.

Planners know they are likely to receive more recognition and job security when they complete current gifts or irrevocable arrangements that pay the donor a life income with the charity guaranteed to receive the remainder in the future. Promises of future gifts that may be revoked by the giver prior to death are welcomed, but the pressure is always on charitable gift planners to secure gifts that can be used now. Because the need for current income is so great, management often has difficulty justifying spending budget dollars to encourage revocable deferred gifts that won't mature for three to seven years or even longer.

## GIFT PLANNERS MUST HAVE INTEGRITY

When placed in a position where conflicts of interest may arise, gift planners must first settle the ethical question of conduct. As long as planners are compensated by charities and try to represent both the charities' and the givers' interests at the same time, receiving recognition as professionals will be difficult. What is the answer?

A step in the right direction is for charitable gift planners to understand what prospective givers want to accomplish, then help them achieve their goals by becoming coordinators of the charitable estate- and gift-planning process. By coordinating a team approach, gift planners stay close to the givers, but they do not advise them on legal matters and they recommend that the givers' own advisors be involved in helping them carry out their wishes. By following this approach, charitable gift planners can maintain a safe distance from the technical decisions and plans of their givers. Others do the work of carrying out the givers' wishes. Charitable gift planners are not financial planners but are able to assist prospective planned givers in the most effective ways possible as they make voluntary gifts while they live and after death.

## GIFT HARVESTING: ONE APPROACH TO CONFLICT

The best position for the leadership of the nonprofit organization is always to put givers' interests first, and mean it. At the Mayo Clinic, in Rochester, Minnesota, a statement by Dr. Charles Mayo at the entrance of one building reads: "The need of the patient comes first." Charitable gift planners and their trustees may want to adopt a similar position. Shouldn't they want to offer voluntary givers the same consideration the Mayo Clinic offers patients?

To deal with ethical questions that arise, charitable gift planners and their managements must develop a philosophical statement on "gift harvesting" that everyone concerned adheres to. Think of the two extremes that now exist in the charitable gift planning "marketplace." One charitable gift planner may be thinking "I work for a fine institution that serves people in an area of great need and I will do anything I need to do to get the money to make this institution survive and grow." Another charitable gift planner who is at the other end of the spectrum may say, "I work for a fine institution that serves people in an area of great need, and I will sit down and just wait for the money to come flowing in." Both extremes are wrong. As the pendulum swings from one side to the other, comfortable ground can be found somewhere near the middle. The first questions to ask in deciding these philosophical problems are as follows: Do we believe people really want to give or not give? Or do we need to do something to them to get money from them? A good philosophy may be built around the idea of helping people give to the institution(s) of their choice while making certain they are not compromising their own needs for financial security and economic freedom. When charitable gift planners have no philosophy of work in place, they are like sailboats adrift without rudders. The main idea is for gift planners to learn what people want to do, then do whatever they can to help them accomplish their goals and objectives.

Very often it is unnecessary to make deferred gift plans irrevocable unless the giver needs and wants tax deductions or has other reasons for doing it. It is best to start with the idea that donors can make gift arrangements revocable. Whenever possible, planners should show givers what the results might be, should they want to make their gifts irrevocable, and then ask them to check with counsel before acting. Some management people have pushed planned giving executives to do all they can to make planned gifts irrevocable so they will be sure the donor can't "back out" of making the gift. Charitable gift planners will serve their prospective planned givers well if they will think of them as their own parents or grandparents and assist them accordingly. Then the planners will be on solid ground when considering whether or not the gift should be revocable or irrevocable. Putting donors' interests first will, to a large extent, take away the need for charitable gift planners to spend much time and money learning how to zero in on "making the ask" or "closing the gift." Charitable gift planners then can discontinue the use of revolutionary fund-raising tactics and replace them with the softer and more gentle evolutionary giving approaches. Then they will become the harvesters of voluntary gifts and gather in season. In this way, those who carry out the mission of the institution—people such as teachers, preachers, nurses, social workers, and doctors—become the real fund raisers.

Charitable gift planners can serve prospective planned givers by coordinating the charitable estate- and gift-planning process for them. Then highly qualified regular givers will begin to identify themselves as prospective planned givers. As the result of this process, charitable gift planners can help people give more effectively to the institution(s) of their choice. They then can help them give without endangering the givers' own financial security. They can present optional plans that may provide tax deductions while givers make voluntary gifts. They can assist them in reducing the out-of-pocket cost of giving.

Charitable gift planners can help donors make the gift of a lifetime and work with their institutions as they provide recognition and suitable memorials for those who give and/or for their loved ones. These planners can help prospective planned givers understand the need always to seek the advice of their own professional advisors. By so advising prospective planned givers, charitable gift planners and their institutions will be less likely to be accused of overreaching or being involved in the unauthorized practice of law.

## ARE CHARITABLE GIFT PLANNERS "SELLING" GIVING PLANS?

Another step in making charitable gift planning a profession is related to the first. Charitable gift planners can urge their management to discontinue "selling" irrevocable trusts and gift annuities as commodities or financial products with tax advantages and start building relationships through well-devised communications programs focused on prospective planned givers' need to give. Too often charitable gift planners have been seen as purveyors of schemes with tax advantages that supposedly will cost donors little or nothing. It is possible some institutional leaders, by being the beneficiary of gifts, have not done enough to help make charitable gift planning a profession. Well-intentioned but uninformed leaders have squandered opportunities to build indigenous planned giving programs by buying into ideas presented by some planned giving consultants and financial planners to "Let us do your planned giving work for you, it will cost you nothing." Management that takes shortcuts by becoming dependent on planned giving consultants and financial planners to do the work of planned giving for them is allowing outsiders to work with its major donors, the charitable institution's most important asset.

Charitable gift planning will begin to become a profession when gift planners: (1) know when they don't know, but (2) know who does know, and (3) know enough to call in those who (4) know to give professional advice to others, without being afraid they will lose the gift.

# 9 ▼ The Giver and the Charitable Institution Connection

We have discussed who makes planned gifts, why they make planned gifts, when they give, and what they give to fund planned gifts. We also have looked at who helps them make planned gifts. Now let's approach matters from the other side and look at how charitable gift planners find prospects who are likely to make planned gifts.

## ESTABLISH THE FOUNDATION OF THE PLANNED GIVING PROGRAM

First, it is important to make certain the institution's house is in order. Trustees and administrators must consider the institution's vision, its mission, and the case for giving prior to starting a planned giving program or attempting to put new life into an existing one.

### The Vision

The trustees, senior management, and development personnel of the institution must make a conscious effort to understand the original vision or dream of its founder(s) who may have been charismatic individual(s) or a group of inspired people. They were able to communicate the vision to others who believed in what was being proposed. People became interested and committed themselves to the cause by giving time, knowledge, and money. Such dreams or visions usually come in the form of helping people solve problems that need to be addressed. Usually the vision consists of an idea or special way of caring for the physical, intellectual, spiritual, psychological, financial, and other needs of people. An example of a vision would be "Giving every child in Memphis a chance to grow up drug- and violence-free." Visions are not necessarily based on day-to-day realities. (That comes later.) Instead they can be the wishes and dreams that the organization's leadership will somehow make come true.

## The Mission

Once trustees and senior management understand the vision of the institution, they can focus on the mission, which is what, where, and how to deliver help. Before the program begins, many questions about the mission will need to be answered. A clear mission statement will be used to help develop a plan for reaching regular givers, those who will make special major current gifts to get the program moving ahead, and ultimately those who will become deferred planned givers.

The senior management and trustees must buy into the institution's vision and mission with enthusiasm. Planned giving efforts succeed much sooner when trustees and senior management have made gifts themselves and influenced their natural publics to join them in giving. The ideal trustee represents the institution to his or her constituents and encourages them to give.

## The Case

When the senior management and trustees take ownership of the vision and mission, the next step is to decide what their case is for seeking gifts. They should ask, "Why should anyone give to this organization?

The best way to make the case for giving is to build it around prospective givers' own need to give, which is based on their wants and desires and to perpetuate values. The institution's leadership will need to give careful attention to building and maintaining a case for giving that is easily understood by those responsible for communicating it through the public affairs outreach of the institution.

The institution's management needs to determine how it is positioned in the minds of prospective givers. It must ask: Who are we as an institution, really, when nobody is watching? What are people saying to each other about what and how our institution is serving people?

Ideally, the case is built around the vision and mission of the institution. It states clearly what the people carrying out the mission are doing for those served. Educational institutions center their message around such issues as what is special about their philosophy of education and what professors do for students. Hospitals tell about patient care, specialties, physicians, and nurses. Children's homes and retirement communities relate how children and retirees are served. Each specific case should communicate effectively what the charity is doing for the people and their interests.

## COMMUNICATE THE VISION, MISSION, AND CASE OF THE ORGANIZATION

Understanding the reasons why people make major current and deferred planned gifts is an extension of the case for all giving. Since only a small number of regular givers ever consider making major planned gifts, it is important to design a plan of action that effectively presents this specialized message to the few rather than to the masses. A communications program must be designed to inform, motivate, and educate those whom planners believe can qualify as prospective planned givers. But before the search for prospective planned givers is begun, the mission must be supported adequately with an overall public affairs program that includes the plans for a comprehensive financial development and public relations program. Public relations, in this context, is defined as what is done to create a proper climate for giving. Development is the activity involved in completing the gift-making process.

Communication of the vision, mission, and case is a public affairs activity, because both public relations and development departments are involved when seeking prospective planned givers. To learn who should receive an institution's message, planners should look into donor files, where most charitable institutions keep information on interested people who will fund endowments. The public affairs staff, which will include both development and public relations people, needs to design a communications program that draws the high-interest people out of the masses in such a way that they self-identify.

In the beginning of a planned giving program, planners should gather the names and addresses of those individuals who are in some way directly or indirectly associated with the institution. This list will include the names of the trustees, former trustees, surviving spouses of deceased trustees; certain employees, both active and retired; and current and former donors. It is from this comprehensive list of names that the prospective planned givers will be drawn.

By using research and various communication methods

established by the public relations and development staff to discover some qualified prospective givers, it is possible to draw out of the donor list the few who might just be planned giving prospects.

Once these donors identify themselves and indicate an interest, the planner's goal is to obtain an interview. Through the interview process charitable gift planners learn who these people are, why they might be interested in making planned gifts, what they may use to fund their gifts, and when is the best time for making their gifts. Finally, charitable gift planners can help givers and their own advisors determine how to make their gifts.

## TURNING THE DONOR PYRAMID UPSIDE DOWN

In almost all vocations, pyramids are used to illustrate that a very few customers, clients, or others served provide most of the sales and income. The 80/20 rule is used to illustrate the fact that 80 percent of sales will come from 20 percent of all customers.

Many executives of nonprofit institutions use this pyramid image and state that 80 percent of total gifts will be given by 20 percent of those giving. (See Exhibit 9.1.) However, while this 80/20 rule may hold true in business, it does not fit in well-managed nonprofit organizations. So what rule does apply: 90/10 or 95/5? In most cases the answer is—or should be—neither. Some well-managed nonprofit institutions receive over two-thirds of their yearly gift income from fewer than 100 sources; in many instances this equals less than half of 1 percent of all givers. Some campaign experts say that the top 10 sources should give one-third of the goal, the next 100 sources should give one-third, and all the rest should give one-third. A gift source is defined as any current gift or matured deferred

## Exhibit 9.1　The 80/20 Rule: The Traditional Pyramid Shape

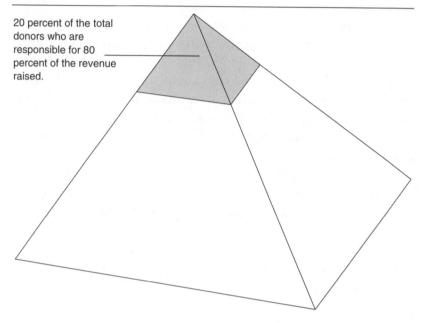

20 percent of the total donors who are responsible for 80 percent of the revenue raised.

gift from an individual or a grant by an association, trust, or foundation, or a sponsorship by a corporation or other entity.

## The Colander Effect

Nonprofit organizations need to consider using an image other than the pyramid to illustrate the location of major givers. Imagine having to pack all the names in the files inside a pyramid and expect to find a way to get to the top prospects who are at its apex. The task of gift harvesting using the pyramid example is very difficult. Therefore, rather than using the pyramid I suggest using a colander—a kitchen utensil found in most homes that is filled with holes for draining—image to discover qualified prospective planned givers. (See Exhibit 9.2.)

The colander idea works this way. Planners should put all present and former donors who are in the institution's universe of names into a colander, then imagine placing a six-sided magnetic wall around the colander. The magnetic wall represents the institution's communications or marketing program directed toward the prospective planned givers. The objective is to attract and draw out of the masses of givers those who may have enough interest to self-identify.

The "drawing" principle is at work here. First-time givers are drawn—attracted—to charitable institutions, and prospective planned givers are usually those who, through a long as-

**Exhibit 9.2   The 80/20 Rule as Illustrated with the Colander Effect**

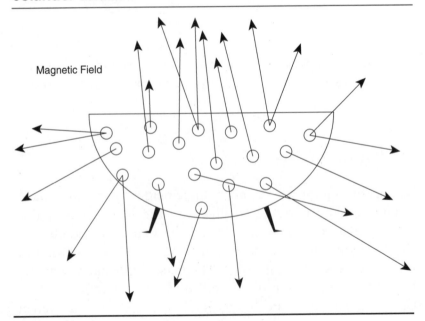

Magnetic Field

sociation, continue to be drawn to the institution's vision and mission; because the institution has a clearly defined case for support, they give. Marketing is the magnet that "draws" them out.

The marketing program can be more effective when it tells the story of the institution's vision, its mission, and its case for giving. The best approach is to work on positioning the vision/mission of the institution in the minds of prospective planned givers and doing it so well that a jogger or passerby can get the message. A paraphrase from the Book of Habakah 2:2–3 from the Old Testament can be applicable here. "Write the vision and make it clear, so those who run may read it." Through written, verbal, and visual communications of the original dream, its mission and case for giving, prospective planned givers are drawn through the "doors" or holes in the colander. They self-identify as having an interest in receiving more information. When this happens, charitable gift planners can extend a hand to help those individuals out of the colander; no longer do gift planners have to climb to the top of a pyramid to reach their best prospective planned givers. Understanding the donors and using the drawing principle can help charitable gift planners reach more qualified planned giving prospects and help them accomplish more than they ever expected to for the institution(s) of their choice.

Think of the famous people in history who have drawn people to them like a magnet. Martin Luther King, Gandhi, even Hitler and Lenin are examples. The mission of the institution is what draws volunteers first to identify themselves as prospective planned givers.

## Easy Does It

When I was in the life insurance business, much emphasis was placed on "making the ask:" asking the prospect to buy the policy being presented in the interview. I was a bit too pushy asking the prospect to buy the policy and then "not let go." There was also a system taught on how to "close the sale." Over the years I have noticed that these terms have surfaced in the planned giving field. Fund raisers sometimes say, "I closed the gift." This is a bit strange, because when we think of gifts we think of opening gifts, not closing them. I've heard it said that "when asking approaches demanding, giving can become taking."

New planned giving executives sometimes bring sales terminology into the field, because they erroneously believe that they are going to continue selling gifts, which become their products and services. This happens because many institutions employing charitable gift planners do not have a stated philosophy for fund seeking.

When prospective givers are approached in a way that helps them identify themselves, charitable gift planners can stop using what some major givers consider high-pressure tactics. While such practices may be generally accepted in sales marketing, nonprofit institutions have nothing to sell to givers other than the satisfaction, joy, or even exhilaration donors receive from giving. Every effort needs to be made to allow givers to respond voluntarily when they consider making major current and deferred planned gifts. Any pushing, pressing, cajoling, or other aggressive, overpowering, persuasive move mars the beauty of making a voluntary gift. The words "Easy does it" need to be made indelible in gift planners' minds. Written marketing materials to prospective planned givers are designed to offer useful information that will help them consider ways to give more effectively. Gift planners should present their case in a way that fits the trustee-approved fund-gathering philosophy. Once people indicate interest, gift planners can begin assisting them and can do so on favorable terms. Then gift planners can motivate and educate them about ways to reach their giving objectives and how to give more at no extra cost or give the same amount at less out-of-pocket cost.

To discover prospective planned givers, gift planners need to communicate the emotional reasons for giving and the concerns for the people being served. As we saw earlier, the desire to give begins in the emotions, but major gift decisions are finally decided in the intellect. What to give, when, and how follow once the donor decides on the who and why of giving.

The best example I can give of how major current and deferred planned giving is done is the life and career of David Dunlop with Cornell University. Dave is, in my judgment, the greatest harvester of gifts in the twentieth century. Several years ago when he spoke at a gathering of National Planned Giving Institute graduates in Williamsburg, Virginia, I asked him: "Why have you been so successful?" He said, "I went to Cornell, I have spent my entire career working for Cornell, I love Cornell. I have the opportunity to meet and get to know some of the fine people who went to Cornell. I walk with them through life, get to know them, learn what they want to do, then I help them do it. I never press them."

# IV WHEN PLANNED GIVER AND GIFT PLANNER MEET

So far we have explored the giver and the gift planner individually. But they could not exist without each other. The next three chapters deal with what happens to bring them together and what happens when they meet.

A whole book could be devoted to marketing, but we are hitting only the high spots here. We show how an estate that includes charitable gifts might be arranged and which planners would take part. We also look briefly at acknowledgment and recognition programs, which are such a vital part of charitable gift-planning marketing.

# 10 ▼ The Charitable Estate-Planning Drama

The certainty of death is usually what causes people to think about planning their estates. However, the ideal estate plan first provides for the one doing the planning during life. It really has more to do with life than with death. Most people want financial security now and later, for their beneficiaries after they die. Working with other advisors, charitable estate and gift planners can show prospective planned givers ways to maximize the use of their assets while they are living, provide for their families when they die, and make planned gifts to their charitable institution(s) during life and/or after death.

Before prospective planned givers can afford to make substantial gifts, they have to make certain they can maintain their financial security and retain their economic freedom. In order to do this, they need to obtain assistance from professional advisors they trust who can help them walk through the charitable estate- and gift-planning process, like those found in Chapter 7. These various advisors can use charitable gift- and estate-planning transfer "vehicles" to help givers make their personal wishes legal.

Estate planning may be defined as the process of arranging and rearranging a person's assets in a way that allows him or her to maintain financial security and retain economic freedom for self, family, and other beneficiaries during life and after death. It is a plan to live by as well as a plan to die by.

Charitable estate and gift planning often is necessary when people make major current or deferred planned gifts. Prospective givers often ask, "How can I make a major gift for delivery now or later without knowing how making the gift will affect my family's overall financial well-being?"

## "THE FOUR Ps"—AN APPROACH TO USE IN THE CHARITABLE ESTATE AND GIFT PLANNING INTERVIEW

The four Ps of this approach are persons, properties, plans, and planners. (See Exhibit 10.1.)

First, givers must list the *persons* they are responsible for—themselves, their spouse, sons, daughters and any others, along with the people's ages.

Second, they should list the *properties* they own—cash, life insurance, retirement assets, real estate, jewelry, antiques, stocks and bonds including mutual funds, autos, and so on. What are they worth now? How much did they cost? How much income do they produce? What is the giver's salary? Are they qualified for social security, veterans', or other benefits?

Third, the givers' *plans* should be outlined. What are their goals? For most people, the first is self-support, now and in old age—living at a respectable level the rest of their lives, whatever their income. What are their charitable giving interests?

Fourth, the professional planners who will assist in the estate-planning process should be listed.

## Exhibit 10.1   The Four Ps of Estate Planning

*For the Estate of*
_____

THE PERSONS IN MY LIFE (names, dates of birth, relationships):

_____

_____

_____

THE PROPERTY I OWN (description, cost, encumbrances, fair market value, income produced—list life insurance policies, pensions, and profit-sharing plans, etc.):

_____

_____

_____

THE PLANS I HAVE (who gets what property or percent of estate—charities to be included):

_____

_____

_____

THE PLANNERS WHO CAN HELP ME (lawyers and other advisors):

_____

_____

_____

Complete this form. *Take it to your own financial or legal advisors and ask them to make your personal wishes legal.*

## EMOTIONAL CONSIDERATIONS OF CHARITABLE ESTATE AND GIFT PLANNING

A number of emotional questions often precede the intellectual decisions in an estate plan. Charitable estate and gift planners must deal with the emotional concerns of prospective planned givers as they make crucial decisions associated with the four Ps as well as the four financial hazards of life. Important emotional questions that the gift planner can expect to hear include the following.

### 1. Who Will Be Appointed Executors and Trustees?

This is perhaps the most important consideration of all. When people start thinking about making their estate plan, some will want a family member to act as executor and/or trustee when they die. The person they first think about choosing to serve may be their father, mother, brother, sister, son, or daughter.

In most families, naming any of these people as executors or trustees probably is unwise. Most individuals do not have the expertise to carry out the assigned tasks, and when the time comes to perform their duties, they may refuse such an appointment. Of course, individuals can act in these capacities, and some will do very well, especially with the assistance of competent trust and estate professionals. The main reason family members should not serve in these capacities is that the executor must make decisions that involve the lives of siblings, their families, and other relatives. The executor/trustee can easily become the "enemy." A poem best expresses this concern:

## THE EXECUTOR[1]
*by Edgar Guest*

I had a friend who died and he
On earth so loved and trusted me
That 'ere he quit this worldly shore
He made me his executor.
He tasked me through my natural life
To guard the interest of his wife
To see that everything was done
Both for his daughter and his son.
I have his money to invest
And though I try my level best
To do that wisely I'm advised
My judgment oft is criticized.

His widow once so calm and meek
Comes hot with rage
Three times a week
And rails at me because I must
To keep my oath appear unjust.
His children hate the sight of me
Although their friend I've tried to be
And every relative declares
I interfere with his affairs.

Now when I die I'll never ask
A friend to carry such a task
I'll spare him all such anguish sore
And have a hired executor.

Many happy families have been broken because the father or mother placed the responsibility on one or even two children who found the appointment to be a burden too heavy to carry.

## 2. How Will Former Spouses and Children of the Marriage Be Remembered?

The charitable estate- and gift-planning process is more difficult when there are former spouses and children of a former marriage to be considered. There may be continuing alimony and child support involved or other emotional ties. While planning itself may not be a problem, the distribution of the assets called for in the plan could be difficult indeed.

## 3. What About Sons-in-Law and Daughters-in-Law, or the Spouses of Primary Beneficiaries?

The actual or perceived relationships between the beneficiaries and their spouses can have a bearing on decisions made by the one who owns the property and is making the plan for its ultimate distribution. The question of the influence of in-laws reaches out into the future and deals with the possible second marriage of a son or daughter.

## 4. Are the Lifestyles of Beneficiaries, Especially Children, an Obstacle?

When a child, for example, is conducting his/her life in a dangerous manner or contrary to the values and standards of the parents, they must consider whether a legacy will benefit or ultimately destroy a beneficiary. For example, if the beneficiary has a substance-abuse problem, they may decide to reduce or delay the amount of their bequest, or the bequest may be made conditionally. Administering such a gift is difficult, but it is the way some people will make gifts to children.

## 5. What About Religion?

The religions of beneficiaries may come into play in some situations. When children marry outside the parents' faith, parents sometimes, in effect, "punish" their children by reducing their gifts at death or omitting them altogether.

## 6. What if Children Are Expected to Go into a Certain Career?

Sometimes the need to control people from the grave may cause a person to make a bequest to a son or daughter conditioned on the child's following a particular profession. The desire to influence events far into the future may cause other estate-planning actions. Dr. Smith, for example, is a well-known surgeon. His father and grandfather were well-known surgeons, too, and Dr. Smith's dream is that his son or daughter, the prospective beneficiaries, will continue the family tradition. It is not at all out of the realm of possibility that Dr. Smith will direct that funds be used to establish the Dr. Smith Chair of Medicine at the medical schools from which his forbears had graduated and, in so doing, reduce or eliminate a bequest to the child.

## 7. Do Presumed Entitlements on the Part of Children Serve as Negatives When Their Parents Plan Their Estates?

Under the laws of most of our states, spouses have legal rights to some or all of the estate of a deceased wife or husband. When people die without wills, trusts, or other contractual arrangements, the laws of descent and distribution provide entitlements to spouses and/or children. (Planners must check state laws.) Some parents believe that children are not entitled to receive the parent's assets upon death, and it is very important to them to believe that their children are able to take care of themselves and that whatever they receive at death is a voluntary gift by the parent. This is especially true when the children have reached majority and are already prepared to build their own careers.

## 8. Are There Additional Ethical or Moral Issues Involved?

Some people make ethical wills as part of their estate plan. For example, the will of a prominent New England businessman read as follows: "To my son: Money is only a goal and not an end in itself. Your grandfather taught me that a man should earn his money until age 40, enjoy it until 50, and then give it away. *The man who dies rich is a failure as a human being.* I say this because I know your abilities will make you a wealthy man materially, but my real desire is that you be rich in heart and soul."[2]

## 9. Are Family Business Interests Present?

They have the potential for creating stressful situations when the founder wants his or her estate plan to assure continuation of a family business by the children. Suppose there are five children and one of them wants to be actively involved. This child has prepared him- or herself to take charge of the business while the founder lives or after his or her death. Three children decided to choose other professions and didn't want to be involved in the business, and the other was not actively involved but wanted the spouse to have a management role in operating the business (but the spouse had no experience in this kind of business). The children own equal amounts of a minority interest in the closely held business, and all of them want to receive dividends. The founder has a strong desire that the business be continued, but he or she wants to stay involved for as long as possible. Satisfying everyone will be almost impossible.

## THE ESTATE- AND GIFT-PLANNING DRAMA AND HOW IT UNFOLDS

The star of the charitable estate- and gift-planning drama is the person whose estate is being planned. The costar is more than likely the spouse. To complete the drama, the supporting cast includes lawyers, trust executives, certified public accountants, life insurance agents, business planners, charitable gift planners, or other trusted individuals. Any of these advisors may become the lead person or coordinator of the charitable estate- and gift-planning process, but seldom (if ever) can one person do everything. More than one legal and financial service executive usually is involved before, during, and after the planning is completed. (See Exhibit 10.2.)

The star's first interest in making a major gift may have begun with a charitable gift planner from the beneficiary institution. This happens because this person's full-time job is to discover and assist those who are already prospective planned givers. However, ethical charitable gift planners do not attempt to do the whole job alone. They advise prospective planned givers to consult with other personal advisors. For example, it can be argued that wills and other necessary documents must be prepared and/or approved by the giver's own lawyer and tax opinions need to be rendered by their own competent tax counsel.

The other characters in the charitable estate- and gift-

## Exhibit 10.2 The Estate and Gift Planning Drama

*The Star: The Gift Planner*
*The Costar: The Spouse*

*Supporting Cast*
Lawyers
Trust executives
Family
CPAs, life insurance agents
Business planners
Charitable gift planners
Securities specialists
Realtors
Appraisers
Others

planning drama tend to have lesser roles in the initial planning stage. Life insurance agents may give advice about existing as well as new life insurance and annuity policies. Realtors can give guidance about real property. Security specialists assist when transfers or purchases of stocks, bonds, and mutual funds are needed. Certified public accountants deal with tax returns, business interests, property, and other questions. Trustees, executors, and custodians may be individuals, but often trust companies provide these services. When family businesses are a part of the estate, business planners often play an important role in the planning process. In many major gift situations, an appraiser becomes an important part of the planning team. Because such a large number of people have substantial retirement assets, retirement property specialists may also play an important part.

Avoiding conflicts of interest when working with people on estate matters is difficult indeed. Life insurance agents, stockbrokers, real estate agents, and perhaps other planners who are paid commissions only when they make sales also find themselves representing both the purchaser and the financial service company. Trusts officers, appraisers, investment managers, lawyers, accountants, and others who are usually paid fees for their services sometimes face similar problems.

Prospective planned givers need the assurance that they are dealing with ethical people when they work with charitable estate and gift planners. Reputable professional gift planners know when they know, or don't know, the answer to a question. They point out who can help when it is necessary, and they freely recommend other consultations with legal and other counsel without feeling threatened.

## WHAT HAPPENS AT DEATH?

At the death of the person whose estate has been planned, attorneys, accountants, appraisers, and some of the other members of the cast will return to the stage. The executor of the will and the attorney for the estate probate the will. The executor becomes the deceased individual's personal representative and begins to settle all obligations to society. The will is proved to be that of the person who has died, all of the bills are paid to anyone having a legal claim, and all accounts made prior to death are settled.

The majority of the estate assets may have been transferred by contract or by trust and will not be a part of the probate estate because these arrangements take precedence over a will. (Planners should check applicable state laws.) These assets also must be accounted for and transferred to named beneficiaries after taxes and other expenses are paid. (Assets that are transferred at death in ways other than through the will are included as part of the estate for tax purposes.)

If the provisions of a trust specify that the trust is to be continued after death or when a trust has been established in the will, the trustee may continue to invest, reinvest, and otherwise manage the trust assets for the beneficiaries. When charitable bequests or trust gifts conditioned on the person's death have been arranged, the delivery of the bequest or the charitable remainder is made to the charitable beneficiary.

Trustees may serve from the time the trust is established until the death of the surviving spouse or at the end of a specified term of years following the death of the trustor. The charity is almost always the last-in-line beneficiary. Many trusts are administered for decades before the charity benefits, but as the result of being named to receive the residue (or remainder), many institutions have substantial endowments today.

## Case Study

Joseph and Elizabeth Freedman are a couple who meets the criteria outlined in an earlier chapter for qualifying as prospective planned givers: They have confidence in a charitable institution, have assets to give if they so desire, can be seen by the charitable gift planner on a favorable basis, and are motivated to consider making major current or deferred planned gifts to several charitable institutions now and/or later.

Who are the *people* in their lives?

Joseph, 59, and Elizabeth, 57, are the parents of Paul, Philip, Martha, and Barbara. Paul, 37, is married to Mary, 33, and they have three children: Paul, Jr., 15, Anne, 13, and Mary, 10.

Philip, 35, is married to Kathleen, 31, and they have two children, Cary, 11, and Jane, 7.

Martha, 33, is married to Timothy, 32, and they have four children, Mark, 8, Polly, 6, Lois, 4, and Lisa, 2.

Barbara, 31, is married to Charles, 40, and they have two children, Harvey, 7, and Leigh, 4.

What *property* do they own?

| Description | Fair Market Value | Mortgage | Ownership | Cost Basis | Net Income |
|---|---|---|---|---|---|
| Business Interest | $400,000 | | (Joseph) | $60,000 | $60,000 |
| Business Interest | 200,000 | | (Elizabeth) | 30,000 | 30,000 |
| Mortgage | 40,000 | | (Joseph) | 40,000 | 5,000 |
| Securities | 1,250,000 | | (Joseph) | 660,000 | 60,000 |
| Home | 400,000 | | (Elizabeth) | 250,000 | None |
| Misc. Assets | 200,000 | | (joint) | Unknown | None |
| Retirement assets | 1,500,000 | | (Joseph) | Unknown | None |
| Retirement assets | 160,000 | | (Elizabeth) | Unknown | None |

Note: Joseph's present earned annual income is about $300,000. Total annual income is about $450,000. They have catastrophic health insurance that would be continued after retirement. He is qualified to receive social security payments upon reaching age 62; however, he may choose to delay his starting date to age 65 or later and receive larger lifetime payments. He owns $790,000 of life insurance and expects his retirement assets to grow to more than $3,000,000 by age 70. The current value of Joseph's estate is about $3,200,000 plus any life insurance proceeds. Elizabeth has assets valued at about $800,000 plus $200,000 of life insurance.

What are their *plans*?

1. To be able to live in the style to which they have been accustomed for as long as either one of them lives.
2. To assist their grandchildren in completing a university education.

**127**

3. To leave a token amount to each child because each is employed and doesn't have need.
4. To make certain Joseph's father, Frank, and Elizabeth's mother, Adele, are adequately cared for.
5. To have a contingency arrangement that will provide for any child or grandchild who has bona fide emergencies and financial needs during life.
6. To retain the freedom to manage their own financial affairs for as long as they choose to do it.
7. To give generously to several charitable institutions because they desire to give back to society part of what they have accumulated.
8. To take advantage of federal income-, gift-, or estate- and other tax savings that are available to them when making either current or deferred planned gifts.

Who are the *planners* who will help them make their personal wishes legal?

1. An attorney whose firm has represented them in several matters over the years.
2. A certified public accountant who has prepared their business and personal income tax returns.
3. A stockbroker who has advised them successfully over a number of years.
4. A life insurance agent who has handled their life insurance.
5. They have had a satisfactory relationship with a trust company and would prefer using the trust company as their executor and trustee rather than placing this responsibility on their children.
6. They have worked closely with a business planner who has consulted with them in the past and whom they would consider using as an advisor if needed.
7. A retirement property specialist who has assisted them in

building their retirement savings plans may also be helpful to them.

They will be able to reach most of their objectives by designing an investment plan they can manage themselves, but they want to provide that, in the event of disability or other problems, others will act for them as their trustee and manage their investments. Documents can be prepared that instruct the trustee to manage their financial affairs and provide other trust services for them or their beneficiaries during life and after the death of Joseph and Elizabeth.

To satisfy their desire to make token gifts to their children at death, Joseph and Elizabeth may decide it is wise to make gifts up to $20,000 per child per year while they are living and also leave something else to them through their wills, trusts, or other contractual arrangements. Doing so may provide significant tax savings.

Joseph and Elizabeth can provide, through a trust or other arrangement, that their aged parents also will be cared for, if they have financial needs now or later.

A contingency arrangement could be made through a trust that gives discretion to the trustee to make distributions to any surviving family member of Joseph and Elizabeth. Since some of their assets are business interests, a business planner and/or appraiser may need to become involved in order to provide advice and/or valuations of the business assets.

They can make charitable designations of what remains in their retirement fund at the death of the survivor of the couple and leave any residue from their wills and/or from trusts they have established.

Through these suggestions, outright or testamentary gifts can be made to designated beneficiaries. Should they want to make living gifts, the first approach to consider may be to give from Joseph's retirement property because of the way retirement property is taxed when children are named as beneficiaries. For example, in Joseph's and Elizabeth's estate, their retirement funds will be taxed at the highest federal estate-tax bracket if surviving children are beneficiaries. In addition, their children would have to pay federal income taxes upon receipt of retirement plan assets.

Here is an example of one of the most advantageous ways to make a charitable gift from a qualified retirement account. Suppose Joseph and Elizabeth wanted to establish a chair in a university by giving $1,000,000 or make a similar gift of that amount for some other purpose, and further assume they want to make the total gift over a period of several years while Joseph's earned income is high.

They could withdraw about $150,000 annually from Joseph's retirement account for the next six years (from age 59 to 65). The gross withdrawal will amount to approximately $900,000 plus interest in six years. If the retirement plan earnings averages 10 percent a year, in six years there would be more than $1,500,000 remaining in the fund.

Under 1997 tax laws, the annual withdrawals are reportable as income but deducted when given. Joseph and Elizabeth may be able to obtain additional tax advantages by using the cash withdrawn for their purposes and giving highly appreciated securities from their investment portfolio to fund their gifts. Under present law (1997) they would be able to avoid any capital gains taxes and deduct the fair market value of the securities they gave.

After Joseph and Elizabeth have carried out their plans for their family, they can name the charitable institution(s) of their choice as the first, second, or last beneficiary for part or all of the remaining estate assets that are left in trust, in contracts, and in their probate estate.

Under this approach, they are able to care for the people in their lives, using their accumulated assets to fulfill their plans with the help of professional planners. By getting to know and understand the people in Joseph and Elizabeth's lives, the kinds and value of the property they own, as well as their plans for using the property, the characters in the charitable estate- and gift-planning drama can help them achieve their lifetime financial goals and objectives. Joseph and Elizabeth can be tax-wise while becoming good stewards of what they have earned and accumulated. Their wishes are accomplished successfully because they turned to trusted professionals who worked as a team and helped them do what they want to do.

## MEETING THEIR OBJECTIVES

As the case study shows, several objectives can be accomplished through the charitable estate- and gift-planning process. Donors can provide for self and family, make plans that will help prevent shrinkage of assets, and save money in the transfer process. They can plan for the orderly transfer of assets by deliberately establishing delays in distribution. By selecting future management, they can help survivors adjust to new lifestyles with more peace of mind. In short, prospective planned givers can decide about the distribution and use of their assets rather than leaving that responsibility and privilege to others.

The charitable estate- and gift-planning process is a complicated one: Gift planners must work around the emotional considerations, intellectual reservations, financial needs, and statutory regulations to arrive at an arrangement that is right for individual donors. Charitable gift planners expecting to receive major deferred planned gifts for their institutions will be more successful when their goal is first to understand the emotional considerations their givers experience when they become involved in charitable estate- and gift-planning. They will be able to assist prospective planned givers after they help them think through the important emotions they face. As mentioned earlier, giving is a response that begins in a person's emotions. Large gifts are not completed, however, until the intellect approves of the amount, the timing, the assets to be given, and the vehicle of transfer that is to be used to complete the gift.

## Notes

1. Edgar Guest "The Executor," in *A Collected Verse of Edgar A. Guest, Memorial Edition*. Chicago: The Reilly & Lee Co., 1934.
2. From Rabbi Ruben Kimelman, *Guides to Personal Growth and Ethical Wills*. National Jewish Resource Center, New York.

# Acknowledgments, Recognition, and Memorials

The establishment of a recognition and memorial program is crucial to the future success of any institution's planned giving effort. A carefully devised acknowledgment procedure is just as important. This is just as true when the program has been in existence for years as it is for one that is now being launched. It is important to have a written plan for acknowledging all gifts. Who is responsible for saying "thank you" and for deciding the way gifts will be recognized or memorialized?

Acknowledgment plans should include carefully thought out ways of determining when special recognition is to be given to certain givers. Recognition and memorial opportunities that can be offered to interested people should be created. When people establish memorials, there is the opportunity for those who give to accomplish two things with one gift. First, recognize the giver, and second, memorialize others.

The three most meaningful words in charitable gift-planning work are research, judgment, and work. Donor research that is bathed in good judgment can be used to help management offer the most suitable type of recognition, memorial, and acknowledgment in each situation. Smart work is required of those acknowledging, recognizing, and memorializing key donors.

All of those who give are special in one way or another. Some of the largest givers are "priceless originals" and deserve special treatment.

## THE ALL-IMPORTANT FIRST STEP

Acknowledgments may range from simple printed thank you notes to personal visits by the chief executive officer. The ideal way to thank most people will be found somewhere in between these two extremes.

Acknowledgments may need to be ongoing, even for the same gift. This is necessary because the first gift is probably not the last nor the largest gift a well-cared-for donor can or will make to the institution. Acknowledgments need to be made promptly and include information the giver will need when tax deductions are claimed. For example, if a donor supports an event by sponsoring a table of 10 for $1,500, the recipient institution should quickly send a receipt for the tax-deductible amount indicating any value received for the dinner. This social event may be just what is needed to whet the interest of the one providing the table and possibly even the guests. Through further contact, a substantial gift could result.

Just as the idea of making a major gift begins in the emotions, it is important to understand that recognition and memorials are motivations centered there too. But before substantial memorial and recognition gifts actually are funded, the intellect is very much involved.

## MAKE ACKNOWLEDGMENTS A PRIORITY

Throughout the years I have worked with managements of charitable institutions and have observed many acknowledgment/recognition/memorial programs in action. One institution acknowledges special gifts by preparing a board of trustees' resolution of appreciation, to be given to these special donors. The resolution is signed by the chief executive officer and the chair of the trustees, and the two of them, ideally a staff person and a trustee, arrange an appointment to personally deliver this resolution in a frame suitable for display in the home or office of this special person.

Another institution has an occasional induction meeting of those who have advised the leadership that they have included the institution as a beneficiary in their wills or other estate transfer arrangements. Each year this institution gives all its donors the opportunity to identify themselves as planned givers; many have responded.

The CEO of one institution my family supports calls within a week after a gift is made. As a result, over the past eight years I have become closer to and more interested in this institution. It has a well-organized acknowledgment system of receipts and letters, but nothing is as impressive as this CEO's one-minute telephone call. Several other institutions we support also have made us feel that our gifts are more important to them than we think they are. Unfortunately, however, most institutions to which we give are not careful in acknowledging their gifts. A handwritten note by the development officer at the end of a computerized thank-you letter is not appreciated as much as a call from the CEO, selected trustees, or program people such as physicians, teachers, pastors, and others.

The CEO who isn't involved in thanking donors by mail, telephone, and in person is probably not using his or her time properly. Making three to five telephone calls a week to thank the largest donors for their gifts should be a top priority. The conversations need not be lengthy but should include an introduction that tells who is calling, why the call is being made, and simply says thank you for their gifts. When CEOs start thanking key givers regularly, some will be surprised and others will be amazed; as a result, they will continue giving, perhaps even increase the amount.

## HONOR, RECOGNITION, AND MEMORIAL GIFT PROGRAMS

If there is any doubt about the importance of recognition and memorial gifts, look around. Churches, schools, children's homes, retirement centers, and other organizations of all kinds place the names of those who gave in conspicuous places.

A person's name is the most important word in any language. Gift planners must handle people's names with care when gifts are acknowledged, recognized, and memorialized. Recently a couple gave money to the Memphis Museum Systems IMAX Theater in honor of their nine grandchildren, and each of their names was inscribed on the arm of a seat. All of these grandchildren were very interested in seeing their names on "their" seats. To illustrate the importance of a name, one of the grandchildren, age eight, cried when he saw that a vandal had removed his nameplate from the arm of the seat.

## CONCLUSION

How important is recognition? Many people work in jobs where the paycheck is the only form of recognition they ever receive. Effective leaders know how important it is to give recognition. The same holds true for the leadership in a charitable institution. Most people want to be thanked for their gifts, some want recognition, and a few want to be memorialized. The next time you make a gift, see how you feel about the recognition you receive or don't receive. Some people gain recognition for themselves through establishing memorials in the name of someone else. These gifts are almost always the largest gifts institutions receive, and they are more likely to be received by charities that master the art of acknowledging gifts. Some people give more because of recognition.

In this chapter, the discussion has centered around acknowledging, recognizing, and memorializing those who make gifts to pay for the ongoing operations of the institution. This may seem out of place in a book about planned giving. The emphasis is because those who make even the smallest memorial gifts are better-than-average prospects for making a major gift through a will or other estate-planning arrangement. The fact that they are properly thanked and recognized for the small gifts they make tends to assure them that they are "safe" in making their final gift to the institution, which may be included in a will or other estate plan.

# V ▾ THE ORGANIZATIONAL STRUCTURE AND PLANNED GIVING

While this part comes after the sections on the planned gift, the giver, and the gift planner, it could have come first. It concerns the support of the planned giving program by the board of trustees, the chief executive officer, and other senior managers—a subject arguably deserving of highest priority. Without their cooperation, participation, and ownership, the planned giving program is not likely to succeed.

In the pages ahead, all of these managers and leaders will find information that will help them understand their role in building a successful planned giving program. Planned giving is, of course, a team effort. In order to serve prospective planned givers well, all members of the board of trustees and the management team must become enthusiastic and supportive partners.

# The Role of the Board of Trustees in Making the Institution's Planned Giving Program More Effective

The selection of the board of trustees has great bearing on the stability and growth of every charitable institution. This is true because trustees have more to do with the success of a planned giving program than anyone else associated with the institution. Why? The board is able to set the stage for giving as no one else can. Also, among its many critically important duties is electing the chief executive officer who will represent the board members to the public and to the staff.

## WHO SHOULD BE TRUSTEES?

Trustees hold and manage property that is owned by someone else. Trustees may act as agents and custodians of others' property. They have the legal responsibility for the financial well-being of the charitable institutions they serve. Charitable institution trustees are almost always uncompensated individuals who are elected to serve for a term of years; they usually are invited to serve because they care about the mission of the institution and represent publics that are likely to support it financially and in other ways.

In nonprofit organizations, trustees often are the keys to receiving major current and deferred planned gifts, and they are of great value in helping management acknowledge, recognize, and memorialize those who give. The best sources of new trustees for most institutions is the file of those who give. Nongivers usually do not make effective trustees because they are not involved enough to empathize with the mission and the people in the organization. In fact, nongivers who serve as trustees can become liabilities to those responsible for securing regular, special, and ultimate gifts. Members of the board of trustees need to be able to give and willing to encourage others to give.

Whether trustees give to the institution on whose board they serve has a bearing on prospective planned givers' decisions to give. A common question asked gift planners is "Do all of your trustees give financial support to your institution?" No financial development executive responsible for seeking gifts from private sources should ever have to say no or I don't know to such a question.

Recently, while serving on the board of trustees of a significant local institution, a trustee was asked to make a challenge to the board of trustees to give. He responded later by offering to give $50,000 if all of the trustees made gift commitments. This trustee knew how deeply some significant givers feel about 100 percent trustee participation in giving. While the amount of the gift is important, the simple act of giving by all trustees may be more important in the long run, because when those responsible for seeking gifts are able to tell prospective givers that all trustees give, a great impact is made.

Trustees who are appointed by governments to serve on boards of city-, state-, or county-supported institutions may be exceptions to this rule. Such trustees consider that they are paying their dues by giving their services and feel giving is not called for in their appointments. However, these trustees can encourage voluntary giving by others by setting an example of making a personal gift. The gift does not have to be large, but it will strengthen the hands of those seeking gifts of all kinds when they can boast that all members of the board of trustees have already made a personal gift commitment.

## OWNERSHIP OF THE PLANNED GIVING PROGRAM

If the board of trustees believes a planned giving program is important to the future of the institution, it will select a chief executive officer who understands the importance of having a successful planned giving program. The CEO who is elected must join the trustees in taking ownership of the institution's planned giving program. Unless the board of trustees and the CEO both have something to lose if the planned giving effort is unsuccessful, other priorities probably will cause them to spend their energies elsewhere.

Here are some steps the board of trustees can take to help the institution have a successful ongoing planned giving program.

**1.** Trustees must understand the institution's philosophy for acquiring gifts and make certain it is understood and shared by the CEO and other managers, especially the financial development officer and the planned giving staff. For example: Will the staff be expected to do anything short of stealing to get money to fund the mission of the institution? Will the staff sit around and wait for people to bring or send major current or deferred planned gifts to the institution? The real questions are these: Is the development staff going out to see people to *get* their money or to *help* people make voluntary gifts? The trustees and the management need to agree where the institution finds itself between these two extremes. A clear-cut philosophical statement about how the institution will secure gifts will strengthen the hands of gift planners as they seek financial support for the institution.

**2.** Trustees must make certain it is feasible for the institution to have a planned giving program. They must ask lots of questions. What are the legal considerations? Who will manage the program and who will be served? Why should this institution have a planned giving program and how important is it to those who give? What kind of planned giving program does this institution need? What will the planned giving staff do for the constituents and what will their efforts accomplish for the institution? What will it cost annually? How much patience do the trustees and management have, and can they wait three to seven years for the maturities of deferred gifts? Is the institution at a place in its existence when there are enough mature donors to justify having a properly staffed and adequately funded major current and deferred planned gift initiative? What plans of giving will be used in the program? Will the institution receive gifts in trust and act as a trustee? What will the investment policies be for handling deferred gifts? Are the trustees *really* willing to help make the program succeed? Will they set the example by giving regularly themselves, by being willing to refer prospective planned givers, and by contacting them alone or with an institutional executive? When will the institution begin to receive income it can use from the program? What part of future budgets is likely to be funded with matured planned gifts? Are there board-approved gift acceptance policies in place? Is there an approved plan for acknowledging gifts and giving recognition to those who give? Is there an approved list of memorials for which the staff can seek funds? The trustees need to ask these and many other questions before beginning a major current and deferred planned giving program.

**3.** Trustees must establish policies to help the management deal with relationship opportunities with financial service companies, their employees or agents or suppliers. As a general rule, institutions should not provide lists of donors to anyone, nor should they place the trustees in the position of giving an implied endorsement of any product or individual or vouching for the stability of any business organization. Trustees need to determine their level of comfort in dealing with others who are in positions to influence major current or deferred planned gifts.

**4.** Trustees must consider their policy on doing business with vendors or professionals whose principals are trustees of the institution. In some instances it may not be avoidable, but in others it can and should be avoided. Full disclosure of what is happening is always a must. Vendors' "gifts" can be troubling for a charitable institution's leadership. Sometimes institutions solicit vendors for gifts, which can make bargaining by the purchasing executive difficult. If any business is done with its trustees, it needs to be fully disclosed. Organizations should consult legal counsel when participating in these transactions.

**5.** Trustees need to take ownership of the organization's mission. They will want to know as much as they can about the institution and be able to communicate the original dream or vision of those who founded the institution, its history from the beginning, what the institution does for those it serves, and the institution's case for giving.

## PROFILE OF A TRUSTEE OF A CHARITABLE INSTITUTION

Here are some ideas to consider when selecting members of the board of trustees of a charitable institution. Good board makeup underlies every successful planned giving effort.

THE ORGANIZATIONAL STRUCTURE AND PLANNED GIVING

**1.** The candidates first will have a desire to serve on the board of trustees and will possess the background and experience needed. They probably should not serve on more than two other trustee boards at the same time, unless they have the freedom from business and/or family obligations to give an extraordinary amount of time, knowledge, and financial support to additional institutions. Some retired individuals can serve more than three institutions as trustees with ease.

**2.** They will lend their names and influence to the institution and should have a history of giving their time, knowledge, and money to this and other institutions. They will make regular gifts, at least annually, to the institution and urge those they influence to join them in giving.

**3.** They will be able to influence a part of the institution's public not currently being reached effectively and are willing to introduce the institution's mission to them. In addition, they may be able to help management expand present constituencies.

**4.** They will attend meetings, serve on committees, and become public advocates for the institution representing it to their natural publics.

**5.** They will take the time to understand the mission of the institution and get to know the people who carry it out.

**6.** They will agree to serve a minimum and/or maximum time as a member of the board of trustees. As responsible trustees they will not seek to serve in perpetuity and will assist the governance committee by recommending candidates to be considered as their replacements.

**7.** They will serve with enthusiasm. Serving as a trustee of a charitable institution is a rare privilege that few people ever have. It has been a privilege for me to serve on local and national boards of trustees. The experience has been exciting, and I have been able to make a contribution that I believe will be lasting. For almost four decades I have traveled extensively working closely with trustees of charitable insti-

146

tutions of all kinds and have thoroughly enjoyed it, but I have received more satisfaction from serving as a trustee on a few boards than anything else I have done. Serving as a trustee has made it possible for me to make a contribution locally and have the opportunity to help look after "the welfare of my city, for in its welfare, I will find my welfare" (from the Bible, Jeremiah 29:7).

# The Role of the Chief Executive Officer and Senior Managers in Building a Planned Giving Program

The board of trustees elects the chief executive officer, who assumes the responsibility for the total operation of the institution. (See Exhibit 13.1 for a detailed chain of command.) I suggest that the overall management under the level of chief executive officer be divided into three divisions that are managed by three senior staff executives. They work together and seek to achieve the goals and objectives of the chief executive officer. These three executives are in charge of the following:

- The CEO. This person is elected by the board of trustees to direct the mission of the charitable institution.
- Program affairs officer. This person is responsible for executing the mission of the institution (e.g., the dean of a college or the program director in a children's home or the field director of a foreign missionary enterprise).
- Public affairs officer. This person is responsible for communicating the vision, mission, and case to all publics of the institution, using public relations, which as planned giving is concerned, means creating a climate for giving and doing what is necessary to help people feel good about the gifts they already have made. In addition, the public affairs officer is responsible for the comprehensive financial

## Exhibit 13.1  Organizational Chart

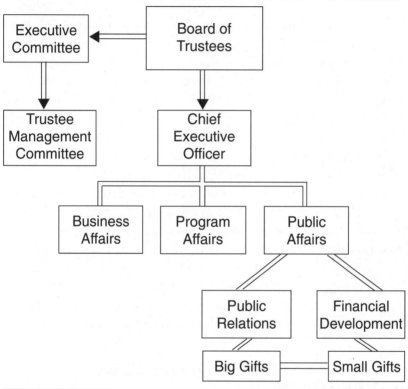

development program of the institution, which seeks gifts, large and small, planned or unplanned.

- Business affairs officer. The executive in this area may be called the chief financial officer, comptroller, or treasurer, and is responsible for taking care of the funds received and dispensing them according to established policies. This person has the responsibility for good stewardship of all of the institution's financial resources.

In some institutions, other senior executives may have substantial responsibilities and report to the chief executive officer. In others, only one or two persons may report to the CEO. The size of the institution has much to do with the number of senior staff.

In order to build an effective planned giving program, the board of trustees, chief executive officer, business affairs, public affairs (financial development and public relations) officer, and program affairs officer must cooperate and become a working team, with each having a clearly defined role in building the institution's major current and deferred planned giving program. They desperately need each other's understanding and cooperation if they and their institutions are to survive and grow. (See Exhibit 13.1.)

Charitable institutions exist because program people care for people and projects. Without these programs, there is no need for chief executives, businesses, public and program affairs, boards of trustees, or charitable gift planners. Moreover, program directors would soon be without jobs if they didn't have the support of all department heads in institutions. Ultimately, one division is not more important to the success of the institution than another. All three are interdependent.

## THE CHIEF EXECUTIVE OFFICER'S ROLE IN PLANNED GIVING

The chief executive officer has a very important role in the success of a planned giving program. The first step is to secure the approval of the program, then obtain financial support from all trustees. If practical from a management point of view, the CEO can be helpful in seeking gifts from the employees. While the amount of money given by employees may not be a significant part of the budget, when employees and trustees give, it sends a powerful message to individuals, corporations, foundations, and others contacted that this is a group of committed people who are interested in being involved in the mission of the institution. The CEO also will be involved by referring prospective givers, accompanying planned giving executives on carefully selected interviews, personally contacting prospective planned givers, and following up with expressions of appreciation by mail, by phone, in person, or in any other way to express the appreciation of trustees and others concerned.

Some chief executives may feel they are too busy and that follow-up is the job of charitable gift planners and others. When an institution has a major current and deferred giving program that is human relations–centered, the CEO needs to be in touch with some of those who may give and especially with those who have already given. Institutional leaders, who depend on many small gifts received by mail, may think that personal contact is not important enough for them to spend their time in this way. Based on experience, this is not true because the importance of telephone or personal contacts by the CEO, even if it is just to say thank you, is invaluable. When the chief executive officer is not involved in harvesting gifts, others who have less influence and who in some instances will be less effective will have to do the job. The CEO ultimately is responsible to the trustees for the success or failure of the nonprofit institution's fund-gathering initiatives. A few carefully selected contacts made by the CEO can mean the difference between having a surplus or a deficit.

## THE PROGRAM AFFAIRS EXECUTIVE'S ROLE IN PLANNED GIVING

If any one of the executives involved in carrying out the mission of a charitable institution is more important to its success than the others, it is the person in charge of program affairs. Without an effective program, nothing else really matters. The job of the program affairs executive is to carry out the institution's mission. Some examples of this position are the deans and provosts of academic programs; directors of hospital staffs, homes for children, retirement communities, community service agencies, religious organizations; priests, pastors, and rabbis; and musicians and directors of symphony orchestras and ballets. These are some of the staff people who provide givers with a reason to give. They are the real fund raisers.

## THE PUBLIC AFFAIRS EXECUTIVE'S ROLE IN PLANNED GIVING

The person in charge of public affairs is responsible for all of the public relations and financial development activities of a charitable institution. This person is responsible for communicating the institution's vision, mission, philosophy, and case for giving to all of its constituents. The thrust of the public relations staff is to create the atmosphere for giving, causing people to feel good enough about the institution's mission to give the first time and keep on giving in the future. The work of the financial development staff members, who report to this executive, is to help complete gifts of all kinds. Since the primary subject of this book is planned giving, most of the emphasis here will be on securing major current and deferred planned gifts that require the assistance of another person. In order for planned giving executives to become successful in what they do, the public affairs executive must join the trustees and the CEO in taking ownership of the planned giving program by giving full support to the planned giving staff. The public affairs executive must know enough about planned giving to ascertain whether the program is operating within approved guidelines and is following the philosophy of the trustees and senior management as well as the trustee-approved gift acceptance policies. The success of the planned giving program depends to a great extent on the leadership of the public affairs executive, who can support the planned giving executive by keeping important elements of the institution's planned giving program up to date and securing the cooperation of the business affairs and program affairs executives. Here are some ways public affairs executives can help.

1. They should make the institution's philosophy of fund gathering central in the thinking of trustees and the other executives in the institution. They must decide: "How far are we willing to go to acquire gifts?"
2. They must keep up-to-date gift acceptance policies in place that are approved by the trustees.
3. They must continue to keep the original vision and a clear statement of mission of the institution in front of all who are in contact with those who give for the support of the institution.
4. Executives in charge of public affairs also should do anything else necessary to communicate effectively the mission of the institution to the general public and to those who give their time, knowledge, and money to support it.

The director of public relations, who serves under the executive in charge of public affairs, is responsible for the public relations program. It needs to be well planned and executed in a way that sets the stage for building an effective, comprehensive financial development program that produces gifts, grants, and sponsorships to support the mission of the institution. In addition, the public relations staff must "buy into" the trustees' philosophy of fund gathering. Nothing is more destructive to an institution than having a public relations thrust that tends to be too pushy. It is also important for the public relations staff to know about the policies for accepting gifts, acknowledging gifts, giving recognition, and establishing memorials.

The public relations program is designed to prepare

those who give now to give more later and to seek those who will become first-time givers. An effective public relations program will open doors of opportunity for all development staff as they seek gifts of all kinds. Charitable gift planners depend on a good public relations program to identify hidden planned givers who might otherwise be missed. For example, the public relations executive may arrange for a series of articles to be written over the by-line of a planned giving officer and published in the institution's newsletter or magazine. The copy can be built around how-to subjects such as giving existing life insurance, retirement plans, real estate, securities, bank accounts, and other contractual assets that may be transferred at death without using a will or a trust. Regular ads could appear in the same publication offering information about including the institution in wills. Such articles are designed to inform and to get people to self-identify that they may be interested in discussing giving an asset other than cash.

While there is much more to a planned giving program than introductory articles and ads, they can help find the hidden givers who sometimes make substantial major current or deferred planned gifts without the knowledge of the planned giving program director. Many people do not want institutional executives to know what they have provided for the institution in their wills. Some will tell management that they have included the institution as a beneficiary but are unwilling to discuss the details. It is wise to say thank you and listen carefully without asking further questions. The will and the voting booth are about all we have left that is private . . . and the will goes public at death. It is best not to ask for details because doing so may be viewed as intrusive and offensive, and may put the future gift at risk. Moreover the answer received is meaningless until the will is probated and the funds are delivered. Thus, I do not feel that the practice of asking about people's wills is beneficial, despite the fact that many consultants, fund raisers, senior management, and some trustees like to count these gifts in their campaigns. When a person notifies the management that he/she has included the institution in a will, the best response is to say "thank you" and start listening for new signals that more contact is desired.

The second part of the public affairs executive role is the institution's comprehensive financial development program. This position includes seeking small gifts and big gifts, both current and deferred. Some gifts are received as the result of mass-marketing efforts, which are closely tied in with the public relations program. Regular giving programs, direct mail, phone-a-thons, television, Web sites, and other mass communication media are used to reach prospective givers. In cooperation with those in charge of public relations, development executives can communicate new giving approaches, such as giving via credit cards, electronic transfer, the Web site, and other methods. Whatever is used to reach regular givers, deferred planned giving should be made a natural part of the overall development initiative. It is easier to build a planned giving program when the public relations staff and other development personnel form a team effort. Most deferred planned gifts will be received from regular, small givers whose wills were made after reaching age 70. One reason these individuals have proven to be better prospects for making charitable bequests than infrequent givers is because they have been thanked more often by the institution's leadership for their regular gifts. Occasional givers are thanked less frequently. Leaders of institutions that have built monthly giving programs made up of many small regular givers may show appreciation a dozen times a year. Not only are these people receiving gift acknowledgments and receipts, they are more than likely receiving other publications that keep the mission of the institution always before them.

Larger institutions are well advised to employ multiple staff members in the financial development department with one person in charge of securing small gifts from the masses and another responsible for securing larger gifts from the few. The small gifts program person may be the key to building a successful deferred gift program. When wills information is offered to the masses of small donors, the institution may learn that this approach is the door to large prospective planned givers. In many institutions only one professional staff member must do all of the public relations and financial development work. Such people will be more dependent on help from the public relations executive(s). Ideally, an institution needs a person who spends full time working in charitable gift planning. Finding the ideal person to handle this part of the institution's development must be a high priority.

## THE BUSINESS AFFAIRS EXECUTIVE'S ROLE IN PLANNED GIVING

The executive in charge of business affairs is, in effect, the steward of all the income and assets of the institution. In many institutions, this position is filled by a certified public accountant who has the same commitment to the mission of the institution and the success of the planned giving program as the trustees, chief executive officer, and executives in charge of public affairs and program affairs. Business affairs executives, who may be referred to as chief financial officers or comptrollers, are as much a part of the mission as anyone else in the organization's program division. Specifically, their function in the planned giving program is to receive gifts, grants, sponsorships, and income from all other sources; to provide proper documentation to givers and make necessary reports to appropriate governmental agencies and others; and to distribute these assets in accordance with policies approved by the board of trustees. In some planned gift negotiations, the business affairs executive is actively involved in the completion of planned gift arrangements. In fact, some chief financial officers take the leading role in completing planned gifts.

The planned giving staff may need the cooperation of the business affairs staff as gifts are being acknowledged and recognized. Any proposed planned gift that is not covered by existing policies should be cleared with the business affairs executive, then the chief executive officer and possibly the board of trustees prior to acceptance. Business affairs officers often are called upon to monitor the use of designated funds and make certain the institution is disbursing funds in accordance with agreements made with the giver when the gifts were accepted. Business affairs executives need to know as much as possible about the planned giving program in order to help those involved in charitable gift planning. They need to become aware of how their expertise can be used to encourage those involved in securing planned gifts and to provide excellent administration of the gift plans after they are completed. The way the gifts are administered will have a good or bad effect on future gift considerations by donors. The business affairs office may be called upon when planned gifts are being completed and as a result may establish important ongoing relationships with donors. Executives in charge of business affairs need to be involved in policy decisions about whether the institution serves as trustee for those making gifts through charitable remainder trusts, pooled income funds, and gift annuities. They have to consider carefully what the gift will be worth to the institution at the projected death of the donor. Sometimes givers will ask for higher payouts, which may leave little or nothing for the charity after their death. It is important for the business/financial office of the institution to determine, in advance, the current value of the charitable remainder interest and to decide if the institution will act as trustee. If it does act as trustee, it is wise for the trustee fees to be charged to the trust as an expense, instead of using other donors' gifts to pay this cost. I have assisted institutions in establishing gift annuity and pooled income fund programs, but it took me years to discover that many of these programs were not very profitable to the institutions. Trustees and management should take a long, hard look at their gift annuity and pooled income fund programs to determine if the number of net gift dollars that ultimately go to their institutions is really worth the time cost and dollar cost of acquisition and administration. These are excellent programs when they are large enough to pay the cost of lifetime administration and deliver adequate gift amounts at death, which the givers expected to provide. However, longer average life expectancies and the time value of money are two important considerations when deciding whether to implement these two programs, and the business affairs executive understands both. When an institution receives too few gift annuities of too small a size, they probably do not deliver many net dollars after paying all costs. Instead of gift annuities and pooled income fund gifts, the planned giving program of the future should first encourage gifts through wills, revocable trusts, existing life insurance policies, retirement plans, deeds to real estate, securities (including mutual funds), and gifts of other contractual assets. When appropriate, planners should assist prospective givers in establishing charitable remainder trusts, charitable lead trusts, and life estate agreements. As a general rule, most institutions should not serve as trustee or pay the cost of administering charitable remainder trusts or appraisals and fees involved in completing such arrangements.

Sometimes major donor prospects want a copy of the institution's financial report provided immediately, on the date of request. For example, I recently received a gift request from an institution that I was considering supporting. Since I have no idea what their financial situation is, I called and asked for a copy of their latest financial statement. The first person who answered the phone didn't understand what I wanted. Later the executive director's assistant said she knew what I wanted and that I would have to speak with the executive director. Two days later the executive director called me and said, "We don't give out that kind of information." I am not likely to make a gift to that institution. Whoever answers the telephone needs to be instructed that the institution's audited annual report is available and will be mailed on the day it is requested. The institution must practice good stewardship and be readily accountable. A donor once told me that because nonprofit institutions exist at the pleasure of taxpayers, they give up their right to privacy.

## CONCLUSION

In order for the CEO and the institution to be successful, the program affairs, public affairs, and business affairs departments need to function as a team. These three divisions are like three trains starting on three parallel tracks. The first train may be an old wood burner, the second train has a diesel engine, and the third train is atomic-powered. The CEO gives the go signal and all three engineers pull the throttles wide open. In a matter of minutes, the trains are out of sight of one another. When this situation exists, the parallel tracks have to be replaced with one main line and side tracks for passing and meeting each other. The chief executive officer is the chief dispatcher who directs the engineers. They may run their engines at full throttle when the track is clear, but they must be prepared to be sidetracked for the other trains to meet or pass. Ultimately all of the trains come together in the railyard, and there, with the chief dispatcher, the chief executive officer, and the owners of the railroad (the board of trustees), future policies are made. The engineers support and carry out the instruction of the owners through the chief dispatcher who runs the railroad company. The most effective planned giving programs are the ones that involve all senior management and trustees in the execution of the program. By having a well-conceived planned giving program, executed by a qualified comprehensive financial development executive, many institutions will be able to dispense with some of their periodic capital and endowment campaigns. Executives can accomplish this by doing, on an ongoing basis, tasks that usually occur only during a campaign. This is possible now because many highly qualified executives can run their own programs with little assistance from outside consultants. Simplification is the key to the success of a planned giving program. Charitable gift planners will learn how to open gifts rather than close them. To do this they will have to be patient by giving big gifts the time they need to evolve. Otherwise, planners are tempted to push too hard, too aggressively, and start practicing the art of "making the ask" on the wrong person. When planners are not careful, they sometimes press the best prospective givers too soon, too much. It is possible to succeed in getting a gift now that can cost the institution an entire estate later. Major gifts tend to evolve over a period of time.

*Planned Giving Simplified: The Gift, the Giver, and the Gift Planner* was chosen as the title of this book because I am convinced that a basic understanding of the kinds of gifts people can make, of the people who make these gifts, and of the advisors and institutions that can help people make their gifts is crucial to the success of the planned giving process. With this understanding, charitable gift planners will be able to build up their operating, capital, and endowment resources and will be vital to their institutions because there will be a great increase in the number and amount of planned gifts that will be made in the future. Charitable gift planners who are employed by charitable institutions are the ones who can simplify the charitable gift-planning process. When planning is centered around human needs rather than tax ramifications and the other technical aspects, more people will make more planned gifts to more institutions than has ever been thought possible. A well-run planned giving program can, in time, help management build significant endowments when they are willing to put the needs of givers to give first. Gift planners will succeed in their roles when they help prospective planned givers make the right gift at the right time to the institution(s) of the givers' choice.

# APPENDIXES
# Some Views on American Philanthropy

#  Philanthropy as I See It

**William T. Wolf**
Philanthropist, Mt. Wolf, PA

There are innumerable motives that lead people to be philanthropic. Some say, "It just feels good to do good." Others may be coaxed into generosity by the fact that their gifts will be subsidized by the federal government through tax deductions. Others claim, "It will pave your way into heaven." Still others (and I am one of them) feel that each of us owes something back to our communities, a kind of "civic rent."

In this respect I've been lucky. The family into which I was born accepted as a self-evident truth that everyone ought to practice philanthropy to the full extent of his ability and capacity. In addition, their (never explicitly stated) definition of philanthropy was quite broad, something like: "any activity that is intended to improve the condition of the recipient(s) and enhance his/their quality of life." All of us—grandparents, parents, siblings, cousins, spouses, children, nieces, and nephews—have accepted this as a "given."

Several consequences, for our family, flow from this. *One* is our belief that a gift of time, talent, and concern is at least as important as a gift of money or property. *Another* is our feeling that a gift of education (or training) is more likely to lead to a permanent improvement in the recipient's quality of life than a gift of immediate necessities—the old "give a man

**165**

a fish vs. teach him how to fish" cliché. A *third* is that our primary focus has been on our local communities and counties, where both time and money can be better targeted, if only because we are more aware of their actual and emerging needs. For the same reason a second focus has been on the individual educational institutions we have attended and those located in our home counties.

All of the above has been made more practicable for me, and my entire family, because we have lived in the same very small town (Mt. Wolf, Pennsylvania) and have worked in a nearby small city (York, Pennsylvania) practically all of our lives. We know the territory.

Sometimes it is possible to see clearly the "quality-of-life" improvements that one's efforts produce. Person-to-person charity has its place. My wife spent untold hours helping a widowed elderly aunt to regain her health, literally to extend her life, improve her home, and make her last five years happy. My brother-in-law and I set up a trust which enabled the daughter of a deceased business associate to go to college. Together with a cousin we provided a home for an elderly aunt whose husband had died, leaving few assets.

But our broad definition of philanthropy permits activity aimed at improving the life of the entire community. This can also be person to person or, sometimes, group to group. An example: Over a period of a full year, during a period of riots, arson, and shooting in our home city of York in 1968–1969, I served as a co-chairman of a Dialogue Committee of the local chamber of commerce. We brought aggrieved members of the black community together with members of the city administration, the police, and the chamber board.

For about three hours each week strong feelings, and equally strong language, were vented. It was not pretty. Near the end, as one evening meeting was adjourning, the (white) chief of police offered to drive home a young black activist (who was strongly suspected of being one of the arsonists). The young man accepted. This was not quite the beginning of a new friendship, but a different, less confrontational climate began to be noticeable in subsequent meetings. It was at that point that we could feel that our efforts had started to produce an improvement, however slight, in the quality of life of our community.

Another example concerns the joining together of several local individuals, including members of our family, in an effort to save the Yorktowne Hotel in York. This downtown hotel, built in 1925, now a National Historic Landmark, was scheduled by 1976 to be sold and ultimately demolished. Since that time, with the infusion of considerable money, the hotel has been thoroughly renovated and revitalized. It is now a modernized first-class hotel, but it also retains all the amenities and ambiance that have always made it the social and civic center for the entire community. However, it continues to need our financial support. My (biased) opinion is that the quality of life of the York community is considerably better than would be the case without this center of activity. This example will probably strike many as something other than philanthropy, but I can assure you that that is exactly what it is—if you accept our broad definition.

Generally, however, my preference is to support, with both time and money, *organized* philanthropic entities such as the United Way and the York Foundation (our local community foundation). My belief is that such organizations are set up, and have the requisite ability, to allocate help where it is most needed and, in addition, to provide leadership in identifying future problems and opportunities, serving as catalysts in shaping effective responses to them. The fact that seven members of our particular family, including both my wife and myself, have served either the United Way of York County or the York Foundation, or both, as presidents and chairmen has been very meaningful for me.

I like truly *voluntary* philanthropy. It seems to me to be more effective, less prone to unintended consequences, and more able to correct inevitable mistakes, than *compulsory* governmental good works. I agree with William E. Simon, former U.S. Secretary of the Treasury, who says, "The government cannot, and should not, take full responsibility for people's lives. It is private enterprise, both in business *and human services,* that sparks the most innovative and valuable ideas that move us forward" (emphasis added).

There is no doubt that, given the complex nature of late-twentieth-century life, governments, at all levels, will continue to have an important role to play in supplementing private philanthropy. My hope is that, as they have throughout our history, the American people will maintain their well-deserved reputation for *voluntary* generosity, both the organized and the person-to-person type, and that our government's role will, increasingly and primarily, be to aid and support such activity rather than to displace it.

# Public Service

**Timothy J. Sullivan, President**
College of William and Mary
Williamsburg, VA

"Public service" is a term currently much in fashion, so much so that it risks becoming a catchphrase. Because it is a term so broad, it is often abused. People can serve the public through a range of occupations, not only through those associated with selflessness and charity work, but also through some associated with self-promotion and frequently vilified in today's public discourse: politician, university professor, lawyer.

I am a university president: a professor, a lawyer, at times a politician. I know the pitfalls of those careers. But those are also careers that have prepared me to speak with at least a little authority on public service. Public service is not a certain kind of occupation but a way of life. In the truest sense, it is activity dedicated to leaving this world a better place for our having been here. It is work—of people acting individually or collectively—that manifests a sense of responsibility for others: a sense of responsibility that transcends individual differences and that binds us each to the other through a shared commitment to the good of the whole.

My colleague at William and Mary, Professor Robert Gross, distinguishes between *charity* and *philanthropy*, at least as the two terms describe discrete historical movements

**169**

within the broader rubric of "humanitarianism." Charity, he argues, "expresses an impulse to personal service; it engages individuals in concrete, direct acts of compassion and connection to other people." Philanthropy, on the other hand, "seeks not so much to aid individuals as to reform society. . . . By eliminating the problems of society that beset particular persons, philanthropy aims to usher in a world where charity is uncommon—and perhaps unnecessary." Professor Gross goes on to argue that philanthropy has become institutionalized to such an extent that we may have lost sight of its source in the charitable impulse: "when we focus mainly on the institutions of philanthropy, the ideas of leaders, and the issues of public policy, we become distanced from the very people who are ultimately the source and the focus of this enterprise: the donors, the volunteers, and the recipients. That . . . is to deprive philanthropy at once of its practical effectiveness and its moral purpose." And so Professor Gross calls for the reintegration of the charitable spirit into discussions of public philanthropy.[1]

If charity work, as Professor Gross describes it, is "private service," then I suppose what I mean by "public service" is what he associates with "philanthropy." A very large and very important component of public service is voluntarism—charitable work—and certainly any public service has at its heart the improvement of the lives of individuals. And so what I mean by public service is not *different* from voluntarism although it is *larger*; it certainly and, as I will argue, necessarily encompasses paid work (even some that pays very well), and it has as its goal the improvement of society itself. I would reiterate Professor Gross's point that to act truly in the service of the public, we cannot forget the individuals involved. But to act in the service of the public, our aim by definition must be broader than the individual.

And so I think of public service as a duty to the public—

one very often performed through the education of the individual. Reanimating our society with the spirit of public service is the most important challenge we face today. And since I am president of a university, you will not be surprised that I believe that task can be best accomplished through education—and through the support of education. In Virginia, we are fond of quoting Thomas Jefferson; certainly one would be hard pressed to find a better spokesman for the interdependence of education and public service. Of all the purposes of education, Jefferson wrote, "none is more important, none is more legitimate, than that of rendering the people the safe, as they are the ultimate, guardians of their own liberty."[2] Education, for Jefferson, was a public service designed to produce public servants—caretakers of the democracy.

But as Benjamin R. Barber argues in a 1993 article in *Harper's Magazine,* Americans have lost our sense of duty to public service—and so our sense that people are not born "guardians of their own liberty" but must be *rendered* so: "We have been nominally democratic for so long that we presume it is our natural condition rather than the product of persistent effort and tenacious responsibility. We have decoupled rights from civic responsibilities and severed citizenship from education on the false assumption that citizens just happen. We have forgotten that the 'public' in public schools means not just paid for by the public but procreative of the very idea of a public."[3]

Barber eloquently reminds us that liberty—democracy—requires the work of the individual as well as the commitment of the community. "Embedded in families, clans, communities, and nations, we must learn to be free. We may be natural consumers and born narcissists, but citizens have to be made. Liberal arts education actually means education in the arts of liberty."[4]

"Citizens have to be made," and it is the duty of citizens

to make them. The goal of education—for Mr. Jefferson, for Mr. Barber, for me—is to create citizens—or, if you will, public servants. Ironically, some of our greatest public servants fail to understand this. Reflecting on his days as a faculty member and sometime dean at Harvard, McGeorge Bundy remarked, "Turning back to the fifties, I will assert that we were right on one absolutely vital point: we knew what a university was for: learning. The university is for learning . . . not for politics, not for growing up, not even for virtue except as these cut in and out of learning and except also as they are necessary elements of all good human activity."[5]

With all due respect to Mr. Bundy, I disagree with him fundamentally on this point: that "learning" remains somehow independent of virtue, of "good human activity." The institution of which I am president—the College of William and Mary in Virginia—*is* about learning, at its most rigorous and rewarding. And it seems to me almost savage to believe that in the university, virtue must be at worst a fugitive and at best an afterthought. The college has a long tradition of educating leaders—like Jefferson—and we pride ourselves on teaching them the *virtue*, if you will, of public service broadly construed. We take our task from Jefferson: "Education," he wrote, "engrafts a new man on the native stock and improves what in his nature was vicious and perverse into qualities of virtue and social worth." The *virtue* of education, its chief purpose, is to "advance the knowledge and well-being of mankind," to render "ourselves wiser, happier, or better than our forefathers were."[6]

And so I assert that public service is not only a service *to* the public but must become once again the service *of* the public. Education creates citizens an individual at a time. But if those efforts are to bear fruit for an entire community—or country—or culture, citizens must work together to provide sufficient resources to create the citizens of the next generation. Public service needs the combined efforts of private giving—Professor Gross's notion of charity—and public commitment—the efforts of teachers, lawyers, politicians, *public servants*.

These times strain human resources to the limit. The problems of the individual, the family, the community, the society seem to multiply exponentially. And at times like these, we often retreat inward, looking to the safety and security of trusted individuals, of family, of the small community. But it is at times like these when we most need to look outward—to create a common sense of the *public* good. At times like these, we must reaffirm our determination to help improve the lives of those with whom we share our common humanity. And in so doing, we discover the paradox of service; that in giving we enrich our own lives.

## Notes

1. Robert A. Gross, "Giving in America: From Charity to Philanthropy," Lecture to National Planned Giving Institute at the College of William and Mary, October 4, 1993.
2. Thomas Jefferson, *Writings*, ed. Merrill D. Peterson (New York: Library of America, 1984).
3. Benjamin J. Barber, "America Skips School: Why We Talk About Education and Do So Little." *Harper's Magazine* (November 1993) pp. 39–46.
4. Ibid.
5. "Bundy on the University." *Harvard Magazine* (January–February 1997).
6. Jefferson, *Writings*.

# Tsedakah

**Rabbi Marc Lee Raphael**
Judaic Studies
College of William and Mary
Williamsburg, Virginia

"Charity" is from the Latin root *caritas*, meaning love, dearness, fondness. "Philanthropy" comes from a combination of two Greek roots, *philia*, meaning love, and *anthropos*, meaning man. So both are originally acts of love, actions motivated by caring for others. *Tsedakah*, on the other hand, is from a Hebrew root that means justice or righteousness, that which is right (Deuteronomy 24:13 and Isaiah 32:17). Surely it includes the feeling of caring, but it goes one step further, beyond whether one feels loving and caring to others, and demands, obligates, commands giving. Philanthropic giving or charity in the Jewish tradition is a *mitzvah*, a duty incumbent on men and women, a divine command that does not leave us to our individual moods but requires us to give no matter how we feel at a particular moment.

Indeed, the Talmud states that "If a man gives even a *perutah*, the smallest coin, to the poor, he is deemed worthy to receive God's presence."[1] The amount is secondary to the act of giving, and giving, in the Judaic tradition, is an avenue to experiencing God. This obligation, and opportunity, is available to all and required of all—even "a poor person who receives *tsedakah* must give from what he (or she) receives."[2]

In many Jewish homes, Jewish children are trained in the ways of *tsedakah* by putting money in a little box (the practice was common in the early centuries);[3] when the box is full, they empty its contents and contribute the money to the needy. The privilege and obligation of giving is taught to children at an early age, with the hope that it will become a regular pattern in each Jew's life. When a young man or woman is a Bar or Bat Mitzvah, at the age of 13, he or she is responsible for the commandment of *tsedakah*.

Many Jews have listed degrees of giving, usually ranking helping someone to become self-sufficient and no longer dependent on *tsedakah* as the highest of all. The medieval philosopher Moses Maimonides delineated such a list of eight degrees of giving *tsedakah* and agreed that aiding someone to become self-supporting (by advancing money or by helping the poor person to some permanent job) is the ultimate goal of giving. Maimonides also reiterated a concern of the ancient rabbis that the poor should never be put to shame by receiving charity.[4]

Although *tsedakah* is a religious concept, a divine command obligating every religious Jew, many Jews who do not consider themselves "religious" are heavily influenced by the emphasis on philanthropy in the Judaic tradition. The various Jewish philanthropies in the world rank high in the amounts of money they collect annually, as Jews, secular as well as religious, have been strongly influenced by the religious tradition of *tsedakah*.

It is rightly said of Jews that they are charitable, and their experience in America began with this theme. When Governor Peter Stuyvesant wished to keep a group of Jews from landing in New Amsterdam (the colony that became New York City) out of fear that this impoverished group would become a public burden, the Jews were able to point to an ancient history of never allowing a fellow Jew to depend on public charity. (In fact, the rabbis viewed charity as a matter

of pubic safety and public administration; they institutionalized it in every community in the early centuries of this era).
So the Dutch authorities ordered the governor to allow the
Jews into the city, and since that time Jews in America have
generously supported both Jewish charities and public
causes of all kinds, beyond their proportion in the American
population.

## Notes

1. Babylonian Talmud, Baba Batra 10a.
2. Babylonian Talmud, Gittin 7b.
3. Babylonian Talmud, Baba Batra 8-9 and Mishnah Peah
   8:7.
4. Babylonian Talmud, Hagigah 5a.

# Stewardship from a Christian Point of View

## Robert G. den Dulk

Stewardship represents the act of caring for what has been entrusted to us. Christian stewardship is the result of having come to faith in the God and realizing all we have belongs to Him, including the earth, the Bible, and all of our resources. In our stewardship we now in thanksgiving give back some of what God has entrusted to us.

Biblical history, beginning with the Old Testament, teaches us that stewardship is to be practiced at every level of life. Stewardship involves money but also includes care for the creation, for our families, and for one another. Genesis 1:28 tells us that man is to "Be fruitful and multiply; fill the earth and subdue it; have dominion over the fish of the sea, over the birds of the air, and over every living thing that moves on the earth." There is to be no abuse of the creation. This passage declares to us that during our life span we are "trustees" of what God has made in the world, of our families and our responsibility for one another.

The Christian's response is living in obedience to God, which includes being a steward. The Christian asks: What can I do to honor God with my life, with His creation, with my resources, and for my fellow man?

Stewardship is not limited to helping other Christians. When someone else has a need, a Christian, as a good steward, tries to meet that need. The Christian steward in a real sense acts as a trustee and understands his or her responsibility to use financial resources to help others.

A rich man came to Jesus one day and asked what he must do to inherit eternal life. First Jesus told him he had to keep all the commandments. Jesus showed him how he hadn't kept the commandments and said to him, "Sell all that you have and give to the poor." The rich man did not want to do that and left a very sad person.

One day as Jesus was teaching his disciples, a poor widow came and brought a mite (a very small amount of money) to the temple treasury. Jesus pointed out to his disciples that this woman, in her poverty, had done so much more than the other people who came because they gave out of their abundance.

Christian stewardship means that when a person is a follower of Jesus and loves his or her neighbor, he or she is going to practice philanthropy to its fullest extent. A Christian does these things not out of duty but out of thanksgiving to God.

The Christian principles of giving were practiced by those who came to America for religious freedom more than 200 years ago. These people were influenced by the Reformation principle that money in and of itself was not bad. It was a good thing when used properly. The Pilgrims who came to America were also influenced by such persons as Richard Baxter, the great English Puritan preacher, who in a sermon said: "If God shows you a way in which you may lawfully get more than in another way (without wrong to your soul, or to any other), if you refuse this, and choose the less gainful way, you cross one of the ends of your calling, and you refuse to be God's steward."[1] John Wesley, the father of Methodism, said to followers: "Having first gained all you can, and secondly, saved all you can, then give all you can."[2] A Christian who has the ability to generate wealth is encouraged to do so, so he or she may share with the person or institution in need.

Thus the background of the Christian's concept of giving is one that calls upon him or her to give out of a willing heart with profound thanksgiving for what God has done for the person. There is no limit as to what kinds of gifts can be made, how much should be given, or the methodology as to how it is accomplished. For one person it may be the giving of time. For another it may be sharing his or her learning or skills. For someone who is blessed with gifts of leadership, it is to lead and direct others. Another person may have great ability in generating money. Some of the large foundations and educational institutions in America were begun by persons who realized they were so abundantly blessed that it was their joy to share what had been entrusted to them with others.

In my experience as an administrator and president of a theological school as well as serving on the boards of various institutions, I find great joy in being able to share my business and administrative experience. We have also been entrusted with a successful business from which we are able to share our financial resources with those who are less fortunate.

In my role as a financial development administrator, I have been privileged to work with donors who, without the desire to be recognized for their generosity, give and give and give. In most of these cases the people continued to be blessed not only with further material blessing but received great joy in what they were doing.

## Notes

1. Leland Ryken, *Worldly Saints* (Grand Rapids, MI: Zondervan, 1990), p. 58.
2. *The Works of John Wesley, Third Edition, Complete and unabridged,* Volume 6 (Grand Rapids, MI: Baker Books, 1996), p. 133.

# The National Association of Colored Women:
## An Example of Philanthropy and Voluntarism in the Black Community

**Tullia Brown Hamilton, PhD**
Executive Director, Community
Foundation, St. Louis, MO

In 1896, two organizations of African American women merged to form the National Association of Colored Women (NACW). A federation of women's clubs, the NACW had as its goal improving the condition of Black women and children through voluntary and philanthropic efforts in the African American community. The creation of this organization unleashed a powerful tide of voluntary and philanthropic activity in the African American community. The NACW did not initiate the concept of philanthropy and volunteerism in the African American community, rather it was heir to a tradition in the African American community that was as old as the country itself.

Philadelphia was the site of one of the earliest recorded examples of philanthropy and voluntarism in the Black community. In 1793 Richard Allen, best known as founder of the African Methodist Episcopal Church, organized Blacks in that city to assist with tending the sick and burying the dead

**183**

during one of the city's frequent yellow fever epidemics. Allen went on to form one of the earliest African American benevolent societies, the Free African Society, in 1796. The society paid death and survivor benefits to its members. Similar organizations sprang up among Blacks in other cities along the Eastern Seaboard. By the 1840s some 100 of these organizations existed in Philadelphia; Baltimore had over 35. Many of the benevolent societies offered services that over time evolved to become schools.

One of the nation's preeminent philanthropists during the early days of the republic was Paul Cuffee. A New England shipbuilder, Cuffee used his fortune to establish a school attended by both Blacks and Whites. Peter Williams's funeral oration for Paul Cuffee eloquently describes the incident.

> In 1797, Capt. Cuffee, lamenting that the place in which was destitute of a school for the instruction of youth; and anxious that his children should have a more favorable opportunity of obtaining an education than he had had, proposed to his neighbors to unite with him in erecting a school-house. This, the utility of the object was undeniable, was made the cause of so much contention, (probably on account of his colour) that he resolved at length to build a school-house on his own land at his own expense. He did so, and when finished, gave them the use of it gratis, satisfying himself with seeing it operated for the purpose contemplated.[1]

Ultimately despairing of the future of Blacks in the United States, Cuffee underwrote the cost of an expedition to colonize Blacks in what is now Sierra Leone.

Other early Black philanthropists include Amos Fortune, who left a bequest that supported a school in Jaffrey, New Hampshire, and Marie Couvent and Thomy Lafon of New Orleans, who also left legacies for schools. Throughout the pre–Civil War era, Black Americans contributed time and money to a host of causes including abolition, temperance, and women's rights.

The National Association of Colored Women's clubs mirrors a number of post–Civil War trends, such as the emergence of women as a force in the social welfare movement and the emphasis on self-help and racial solidarity within the Black community. The NACW paralleled the White General Federation of Women's Clubs (GFWC). When charged with being a mere imitation of the GFWC, NACW members pointed out that White women's clubs focused on the improvement of its members, while the NACW focused on uplifting a race. By 1911 approximately 45,000 Black women were associated with these clubs in almost every state of the union. The heart of the work was at the local level.

Most club activity focused on the needs of children. In 1902 the women of Charleston, South Carolina, organized a free kindergarten. Its aim was to "protect the children between the ages of three and seven from the promiscuous influence of the streets." Clubwomen in Los Angeles also operated a day nursery.

Children who had run afoul of the law were not ignored. In most southern states, little or no provision was made for Black youth offenders. These children were sent to adult correctional facilities. Black women's clubs in Alabama, Texas, Arkansas, Virginia, and West Virginia established reformatories for which they then secured subsidies from state legislatures. Clubs in Kentucky and Alabama maintained scholarships to support young women college students. Some clubs established fresh-air funds to give city children a chance to experience nature during the summer months.

The supposed immorality of Black women was one of the issues that led them to organize. It is not surprising then that "rescuing fallen women" and protecting women at risk of "falling" occupied the energy of clubs. For example, the Women's Civic League of Chicago had as its objective "to rescue and reform fallen women and girls and to suppress every form of vice." Young Black women often were lured from the South to the North with promises of jobs as domestics. These jobs were usually in houses of ill-repute. Clubs in large northern cities often arranged to meet trains from the South and make sure arriving women had a suitable place to go. In 1913 the Kansas City Women's Uplift League established a home for working girls. Club women in Philadelphia provided classes in sewing along with recreation and entertainment for young working women.

Many clubs focused on health care. The Phyllis Wheatley Club of New Orleans devoted itself to establishing a hospital. In 1897 a sanitarium was opened. After the first eight months, there were 8 inpatients and 130 had been seen in the free clinic. The city eventually appropriated $240 per year for operations with the club supplying the balance of the operating funds. By 1902 the club also was supporting a corps of visiting nurses. In Birmingham, the women's club organized a tuberculosis clinic. In 1919 the South Carolina Federation sent $1,000 to the state board of health to care for Black tubercular patients.

The elderly were also a target of the clubs' efforts. When it was revealed that Harriet Tubman was alone and penniless, the Northeastern Federation of women's clubs provided her with a nurse and interceded in her behalf with the federal government for the pension she was due because of her work as a Union spy during the Civil War. In 1905 a women's club in Vicksburg, Mississippi, raised $2,000 to convert an old mansion to a nursing home for the elderly.

In addition to developing and supporting their own projects, clubs supported the activities of others. The Women's League of Baltimore raised $1,000 to support the Baptist orphanage. In Chicago, women's clubs provide support to fledgling chapters of the NAACP and the Urban League. Clubs in Philadelphia raised $10,000 to help start the YWCA.

Perhaps the NACW's finest hour was the effort to save the home of Frederick Douglass in the Anacostia section of Washington, D.C. In 1916 the Frederic Douglass Memorial and Historical Association asked the NACW for the opportunity to address the convention to make an appeal to save the Douglass home. The association had assumed ownership of the home after the death of Douglass's widow in 1905. The home carried a $5,000 mortgage, which the association had not been able to remove. The NACW immediately took up the gauntlet and launched a campaign to raise $15,000 to save and restore the home.

Local clubs were urged to hold fund-raising activities in their respective communities. Sunday school and public school teachers were encouraged to hold special programs on Douglass's birthday so that children could learn something about Douglass and contribute a penny to the fund. Black newspapers and other journals provided publicity about the campaign. *The Crisis*, the NAACP's monthly publication, published a list of states showing the amount that each one contributed to the campaign. Black soldiers serving in France collected $1,000.

By November 1917 NACW president Mary Talbert could write to a colleague that she had redeemed the Douglass home and paid all outstanding debts. The convention of the following year featured a dramatic ceremony at which the mortgage was burned. The home was restored and used as headquarters by the NACW for many years. It is now part of the complex of museums operated by Smithsonian Institution.

The honor of lighting the mortgage went to Mrs. C. J. Walker, who provided the final $500 contribution to the campaign. A rags-to-riches story in the American tradition, Mrs. Walker had amassed a fortune of $1 million through her line of beauty products for Black women. Mrs. Walker was only one of the many remarkable women involved in the NACW. Others included Anna Hudlin, known as the "fire angel" because of work caring for the destitute after the great Chicago fire; Annie Malone, who used her fortune to establish a home for Black orphans in St. Louis, and Anna Julia Cooper, who earned a Ph.D. from the Sorbonne in 1925 at the age of 67.

After 1920, the work of professional organizations like the Urban League and the Ys eclipsed the work of the women's clubs. Today few people know about or understand the importance of the club movement among Black women. Their legacy, however, continues in the growing recognition and interest by the larger society of the potential of African Americans as *partners* in rather than *beneficiaries* of philanthropic activity.

## Notes

1. Leslie H. Fischel, Jr. and Benjamin Quarles, eds., *The Black American: A Brief Documentary History* (Scott, Foresman & Co., 1970), p. 38.

# The History of Giving in America

**Robert A. Gross**
Director of American Studies
College of William and Mary
Williamsburg, Virginia

Two traditions of giving have shaped the practice of humanitarianism in America, from the beginnings of the British colonies to the present. One tradition derives from religious principles of Christian charity, as carried to the New World by the Puritan founders of Massachusetts Bay. The second, embodying the secular heritage of the eighteenth-century Enlightenment, inspires the conduct of modern philanthropy. Together, the two strains express a powerful impulse running throughout our history: a spirit of voluntarism by which Americans have given their "time, talents, and treasure" to the service of others. Yet in important respects, charity and philanthropy face in different directions, and at times, they have been at odds. In that shifting relation lies a central theme in the history of planned giving and a major challenge to its practice today.

En route to the New World on board the *Arbella* in 1630, John Winthrop crystalized the benevolent ideal in early America when he summoned his fellow Puritans to make their colony "a Model of Christian Charity." In that evangelical vision, Massachusetts was to be a godly community, "a City upon a Hill," overflowing with "charity," where people loved and assisted one another as brothers and sisters in

Christ. The fruit of gospel love, charity, was a virtue for rich and poor alike. It involved direct, personal acts of compassion to those in need, not simply alms for the unfortunate but also kind words, considerate counsel, pious prayers. Such gifts bound people together across the social ranks; indeed, New Englanders were enjoined to remember even strangers and enemies in their hearts. Hadn't God "so disposed the condition of mankind," Winthrop noted, so that "in all times some must be rich, some poor, some high and eminent in power and dignity, others mean and in subjection?" Within that great chain of being, Christians must fulfill the providential plan and help one another to get by.

In the spirit of charity, Puritans adopted a set of practices common in the Anglo-American world. Every community felt obligated to take care of its own inhabitants when they were in need. In New England, that entity was the town; elsewhere, as in Virginia, it was the parish. In these small communities, aid was direct, personal, concrete. If a family fell into straits, the overseers of the poor paid a visit, appraised the need, and supplied the necessary goods. There were no general allotments of money, to be spent as the indigents desired; instead, the poor received specific items—so many pounds of beef, pecks of corn, drams of rum—as required.

In the provision of charity, the needy were not stigmatized as deviant nor segregated from others. Not till the mid-eighteenth century did poorhouses begin to appear. As with foster care today, dependents lived with local families and were tended at public expense. Victims of circumstance, they suffered misfortunes that could happen to anyone. So long as the Puritan ethos prevailed, the misery of some was an opportunity for others—a chance to be stewards of God's blessings. "What if God were to refuse his mercy to those of us who do not deserve it . . ." thundered one minister. "We deserve nothing but hell; and shall we refuse to supply the poor with a little portion of God's property in our hands of which he has made us stewards?"

That question propelled another son of New England to pioneer other means of doing good. When Benjamin Franklin ran away from his native Boston to start printing in Quaker Philadelphia, he became the pioneer of modern philanthropy. In the Puritan tradition, Franklin affirmed that "the most acceptable service of God is doing good to man," but he applied that principle in a secular, enlightened mode, picking up on contemporary English models. Rather than spiritual communion, Franklin sought practical improvement in the human condition. He was quick to promote voluntary associations for the common good. Was Philadelphia endangered by the outbreak of fire? Franklin founded the first fire company in America. Did young men with a taste for reading crave an alternative to borrowing books from the local elite? He launched the first subscription library on the continent, still in operation as the Library Company of Philadelphia.

Franklin took an equally rational, progressive approach to the needy. Unwilling to accept poverty as inevitable, he sought to eliminate the condition altogether; he would help the poor to help themselves. In Franklin's view, traditional charity—giving alms—was self-defeating; the money was here today and gone tomorrow, the poor as dependent as ever. But by applying the latest knowledge to practical problems, the eighteenth-century philanthropist would remedy social ills. Franklin's good works were designed to end the circumstances that generated the opportunity for stewardship. In the wake, charity would go out of business.

These twin approaches—charity and philanthropy—were at odds in theory but not in eighteenth-century practice. In the small-scale, personalized city of Philadelphia, where rich and poor lived in the same neighborhoods, where workers and servants ate and drank with their employers, the public-minded citizen could combine charity and philanthropy in the same act. Teaching a man how to help himself, Franklin enjoyed an immediate relation with the beneficiary of his efforts and derived direct satisfaction from the results. Social service was not yet an impersonal act. When Franklin promoted a philanthropic goal, he infused it with the spirit of charity.

Not so for his descendants in Jacksonian America, who founded voluntary associations to meet just about every social need. In this "age of benevolence," Americans seized on the principle of mutual self-help, organizing debating clubs, drama groups, lyceums, libraries, agricultural societies, total abstinence societies, and the like. They also transformed the familiar method of helping the poor. In the name of efficiency, reformers urged the creation of formal institutions—poorhouses, insane asylums, orphanages, penitentiaries—to care for the dependent and the deviant. Some of these agencies were established by the state, others were maintained by volunteers. All came to be guided by professionals employing the latest knowledge to rehabilitate and redeem their charges, albeit with mixed success.

The rise of formal, specialized associations in the business of benevolence threatened the traditional practice of charity, as a good many New Englanders pointed out. Like Dicken's Scrooge, the hardhearted now had an excuse to turn beggars from the door and direct them to the poorhouse. Actually, the comfortable needn't see them at all. Hidden behind closed doors, subject to the ministrations of professional caretakers, the criminal, the poor, the insane became a separate, alien order, deserving their fate. A charitable soul might contribute to their support but at a safe distance, paying the bills of conscience on the cheap. In place of Christian love, complained Dr. Walter Channing, a Boston physician who treated many patients among the poor, there arose a new spirit of "exclusiveness." "If it aims to aid Pauperism, it does so by delegation. It knows too little of the detail of every day want and misery, to feel that it can directly minister to its relief."[1]

Channing's concern was well founded, but charity had not disappeared from mid-nineteenth-century America, nor would the impulse to personal service give way entirely to professional social work. Ordinary Americans of every class continued to help neighbors in need, make "friendly visits" to the poor, enter the "slums" of the 1890s and the "inner cities" of the 1990s to learn "how the other half lives." Nonetheless, a tension developed between traditional charity and modern philanthropy that persists to the present. We can see the dual impulses in the late nineteenth and early twentieth centuries, when Christian reformers like Jane Addams, appalled by conditions in the industrial cities, planted settlement houses in which to live side by side with the poor and gain "an outlet for (the) sentiment of universal brotherhood,"[2] and when the so-called Robber Barons Andrew Carnegie and John D. Rockefeller, prompted by motives of benevolence but overwhelmed by the vast fortunes they felt obliged to give away, created the great philanthropic foundations that bear their name. Ironically, though they were inspired by different impulses, these innovations ultimately worked to the same end. They gave rise to new professions—the social worker, the foundation executive, the development officer—and to a new social space, the nonprofit sector, that have become the staples of our society and our histories.

In the progress from colonial America to the present, the story of benevolence can too easily reduce to a narrative from charity to philanthropy, tracing the rise of professions, bureaucracies, and specialized knowledge in the treatment of social ills. That perspective skews humanitarianism in our culture to Franklin's angle of vision. John Winthrop's "Christian Charity" is lost to view. The consequence is to devalue the significance of concrete, immediate service to others that is essential to personal and collective well-being. Charity and philanthropy need one another; the problem-solving mentality of Franklin, for all its contributions to progress, requires the compassion and humility inherent in Winthrop's ideal. The divide between them remains the burden of our history, shared by Americans in all walks of life. Overcoming that legacy mandates a more complex appreciation of the past.

## Notes

1. Dr. Walter Channing, *An Address on the Prevention of Pauperism* (Boston, 1843), quoted in David J. Rothman, *The Discovery of the Asylum: Social Order and Disorder in the New Republic* (Boston: Little, Brown and Company, 1971), p. 174.
2. Jane Addams, "The Subjective Necessity of Social Settlements" (1892), in Christopher Lasch, ed., *The Social Thought of Jane Addams* (Indianapolis: Bobbs-Merrill Company, 1965), p. 29.

# Glossary

**adjusted gross income**—Amount of income remaining after the expenses of earning that income have been deducted.

**administrator**—The personal representative appointed by the probate court to settle the estate of a person who dies without a will.

**annuitant**—The person receiving annual or more frequent payments from a gift annuity.

**annuity payments**—The annual or more frequent payment of principal and interest to an annuitant or to his or her beneficiary.

**annuity reserves**—The required amount of money invested to guarantee the lifetime payments to the annuitant.

**annuity trust**—See *charitable remainder annuity trust*.

**appreciated property**—Property with a value greater than the cost basis.

**assignment form** (separate from certificate)—A form used in transferring ownership of securities from one party to another. (The stock certificate does not have to be signed when this form is used.)

**bargain-sale arrangement**—A method whereby a person sells appreciated property to a charity at a lower price than the fair market value, with the charity realizing the difference as a gift.

**beneficiary**—A person or organization designated to receive the income from a trust.

**bequest**—A gift of property by will.

**board of trustees**—The policymaking body of a nonprofit institution.

**cash surrender value**—The amount of money received by a policyholder from a life insurance company when the holder surrenders a policy for cash prior to the maturity date.

**charitable estate planning**—Estate planning that includes a provision for a charitable institution to receive a portion of a person's assets.

**charitable income-tax deduction**—The amount a donor can deduct from a federal income-tax return for a gift to a qualified charity.

**charitable life insurance**—Any type of life insurance policy that pays death proceeds or living benefits to a qualified charity.

**charitable remainder annuity trust**—A trust made possible by the Tax Reform Act of 1969. It provides for a donor to transfer property to a trustee subject to his or her right to receive a fixed percentage of the initial net fair market value of the property for as long as he or she lives. Whatever remains in the trust at the person's death becomes the property of the beneficiary institution.

**charitable remainder interest**—The amount a charity expects to receive from a charitable remainder trust at the death of the trustor.

**charitable remainder unitrust**—A trust made possible by

the Tax Reform Act of 1969. It is similar to the charitable remainder annuity trust in many ways, except that the income is a percentage of the fair market value of the property transferred, determined annually.

**codicil**—An addition or amendment to a person's will.

**corpus**—The principal in a trust.

**cost basis**—The original cost of property plus improvements and other expenses paid by the owner during the period of ownership.

**cost basis deduction**—The amount of deduction allowed for certain charitable gifts that do not exceed the cost of the property. (See *cost basis*.)

**death benefits**—Proceeds of a life insurance policy paid to a beneficiary of the policy at the death of the policyholder.

**director of development**—The officer of a charity who has responsibility for the institution's total fund development program.

**dividends**—The amount of money paid each year on a life insurance policy or share of stock to the policyholder or shareholder.

**endowment policy**—A life insurance policy that provides a death benefit of the face amount should the insured die during the premium-paying period. If the policyholder lives to the end of the premium-paying period, he or she receives the face amount of the policy.

**endowment**—A pool of property held by a charity and invested to provide an annual income for the institution.

**estate analysis**—The process of collecting and studying data about a person's property to be used in developing his or her estate plan.

**estate planning**—Planning for the management of all of an individual's assets for the benefit of this person and his or her heirs.

**executor**—The personal representative (male) named in a will to settle the testator's estate.

**executrix**—The personal representative (female) named in a will to settle the testator's estate.

**fair market value**—Amount of money a willing buyer will pay a willing seller for property, with neither being under compulsion to buy or sell.

**federal estate tax**—The tax imposed on the transfer of property to others at death.

**federal gift tax**—The tax imposed on the transfer of property during the lifetime of the donor. This tax is paid by the donor.

**federal income tax**—A tax on income.

**five-year carryover rule**—A federal income-tax provision that permits a donor to carry over into the five succeeding tax years any amount of a gift that exceeds the deductible amount in the year the gift is made.

**forced sale**—The sale of property by a person or by an estate, usually at a price lower than the fair market value.

**gift annuity agreement**—An agreement in which a donor makes a gift to a charity, which in turn provides stipulated annual income payments, for life, to one or two persons.

**guardian**—A person appointed or approved by the court to look after the interests of another person.

**heirs**—Those who inherit someone's property.

**Internal Revenue Service ruling**—A statement defining the IRS's position with respect to certain tax questions.

**intestate**—Dying without a will.

**land contract**—A contract between the buyer and seller of real estate providing for the payment of the unpaid balance due on the transaction.

**laws of descent and distribution**—State laws controlling distribution of property when a person dies without a will.

**legacy**—A gift of property by will. (Same as bequest.)

**legatee**—One who receives property through a will.

**life-estate agreement**—An agreement between a donor and a charity in which the donor deeds real estate to the institution but reserves the right to use or reside on the property for life.

**life expectancy**—The actuarial estimate of the number of years a person will live from any given age.

**life interest**—The value of the interest retained by the donor in a charitable remainder trust.

**limited payment life**—A life insurance policy that pays the face amount at death of the insured but requires that payments be made for 5, 10, 15, 20, or more years at a higher premium than for ordinary life policies.

**living benefits**—Life insurance policy benefits paid to the policyholder while he or she lives.

**long-term capital gains**—The capital appreciation realized from the sale of property (stocks, bonds, land, etc.) that the seller has owned more than 12 months.

**marital deduction**—According to federal law, the amount of money that an individual can transfer tax free to a surviving spouse in his or her will.

**memorial gift**—A gift to a charity in memory of a deceased person.

**net income plus makeup unitrust**—Same as net income unitrust except for the provision that the payments may exceed the stated percentage, up to but not exceeding the amount required to make up any accumulated deficiencies for prior years, that is, years in which the trust earned less than the stated percentage.

**net income unitrust**—A variation of the charitable remainder unitrust. It provides that the trustee pays the donor or other designated beneficiaries up to a stated fixed percentage of the net fair market value of the trust assets determined annually, or the actual income earned, whichever is less.

**ordinary income property**—Property that produces income that is taxed at the owner's regular income-tax rate.

**ordinary life**—Refers to an insurance policy that generally requires the policyholder to pay a level premium each year until death.

**owner and beneficiary**—The charitable institution that has control and possession of a life insurance policy during the life of the insured person. The institution is designated to become the irrevocable owner and beneficiary at the individual's death.

**planned giving**—The making of gifts to a charity, resulting from a planning process that considers the effects of a gift upon the donor's estate.

**pledge**—An amount of money a person promises to give over an extended period of time.

**pooled income fund**—A trust funded by a number of donors, each retaining an income for life. Each donor is paid a pro-rata share of the trust earnings. Each donor's portion of the principal becomes the property of the charity at the donor's death.

**primary beneficiary**—The first person named to receive the proceeds of a will or life insurance policy.

**probate**—The "proving" of a will. When a person dies, the will is taken to the probate court to prove that the will is indeed that person's last will and testament.

**property**—Real estate, securities, cash, or any other type of possessions.

**realized capital gains**—The amount of money received from the sale of property in excess of the original amount paid for the property.

**remainderman**—The person or institution receiving the assets of a trust upon the death of the trustor.

**remainder interest**—The value of the beneficiary's interest after the donor's death.

**residuary**—Property left in a person's estate after payment of debts and distribution of specific bequests.

**residuary clause**—A clause in the will that bequeaths or devises property that is not specifically bequeathed or devised earlier in the will.

**residue**—Property left for the final beneficiaries named in a will after all other bequests have been paid.

**retirement income policies**—A life insurance policy or annuity that pays an income for life, beginning at retirement.

**reversionary living trust**—A trust that is irrevocable for a term of years, with the income being paid to the charity during this term. There is a provision for the property to revert to the trustor at the end of the term.

**revocable living trust**—May be revoked at any time by the trustor (with a reasonable advance warning of the intention to revoke the trust).

**rights of survivorship**—The ownership rights held by an individual whose partner in ownership of property is no longer living.

**secondary beneficiary**—Person named in a will or life insurance policy to receive the proceeds should the primary beneficiary predecease him. (May also refer to an institution.)

**settlement costs**—The cost of settling an estate.

**state inheritance tax**—A tax on a person's right to receive property at the death of another person; the tax is paid to state of residence of the decedent or to the state where any real property transferred is located.

**straight unitrust**—A separate trust from which a fixed percentage of the net fair market value of the trust assets, as determined annually, must be paid to a designated beneficiary or beneficiaries for life, or for a number of years not to exceed 20.

**supplementary contract**—An agreement between a life insurance company and a policy beneficiary or policyholder providing for the distribution of policy proceeds at a person's death or at some point during his or her life.

**survivorship gift annuity**—A gift annuity that is created by a will that provides income for one or two beneficiaries for the remainder of life.

**tax-exempt bonds**—Bonds issued by a municipality. They are generally free from federal and state income taxes.

**tax-exempt status**—Refers to the fact that a nonprofit corporation is exempted from paying taxes because of its charitable activities.

**tax gift**—A gift made to a charity after tax implications have been carefully reviewed for tax consequences.

**term life**—A life insurance policy purchased for a term of years. If the person dies during this term, the beneficiary receives the face amount of the policy. The policy expires at the end of the stated number of years.

**testamentary gifts**—Gifts made through a will.

**testamentary trust**—A trust created by a provision in a person's will.

**testator**—The person who makes a will.

**tier structure**—Represents the way in which an income beneficiary must report the income generated by a charitable remainder annuity trust or unitrust. It gives the order in which the income is reported as earned by the trust. The tier is as follows: (1)ordinary income, (2)capital gains, (3)"other" income, (4)return of principal.

**tithe**—The giving of 10 percent of one's income to a charitable institution. Tithing is a practice found in the Bible.

**treasury regulations**—Regulations issued by the U.S. Treasury Department that interpret code sections passed by Congress.

**treasury tables**—Actuarial, life expectancy, and other tables issued by the U.S. Treasury Department for use in calculating tax deductions for gifts made through trusts and by contract.

**trustee**—The person or institution responsible for the administration of a trust.

**trust instrument**—A legal document that provides operating instructions for a trustee in carrying out the terms of a trust.

**trust officer**—The person in a trust company who is responsible for the administration of property of which the trust company is trustee.

**trustor (also grantor)**—The person creating a trust.

**trust principal**—The assets of a trust.

**unrealized capital gain**—The difference between the current fair market value of some property and the original cost basis. The gain is not realized until the property is sold.

**will**—A person's statement to the public regarding the disposition of his or her property at death.

# Index

INDEX